To My Sister in Law
Margie Melta

For Linda 2008

This is a book we all should
have read 40 years ago. It's
never to late to start over.
Sometime God gives us second
chances (He has me many times)
Joy comes from the Lord. Look for
it. You have helped me so

home | improvement

many times in My life I could
never Repay you. It's nice to
know I can call you my friend
& call you anytime. You mean
so much. I Love you
Lia

9 Steps to Living a Joyful Life

home | improvement

Dayle Allen Shockley

Home Improvement

by Dayle Allen Shockley

©2002 Word Aflame Press
Hazelwood, MO 63042-2299

Cover Design by Paul Povolni

ISBN 1-56722-592-6

Printed in United States of America

Printed by

WORD AFLAME®PRESS
8855 DUNN ROAD
HAZELWOOD, MO 63042-2299

Endorsements for
Home Improvement:
9 Steps to Living a Joyful Life

"*Home Improvement* is classic Dayle Shockley. Once again she has opened her heart and invited us in, friend-to-friend. Reading this book will be easy, but doing the work will be hard. *Home Improvement* offers more than light reading; it challenges us to change. Few are better than Dayle at providing heartfelt insights and practical application in the same setting. This book is a great investment of time for those who are ready for change."

— Cindy Miller,
minister, counselor, Christian educator, speaker,
author of *Challenges of the Heart* and *Character Counts*

"If you have never read Dayle Shockley's work, this is a good place to start. If you have read her writings, the excellence continues in *Home Improvement*. Take this book and a cup of coffee and go hide. *Home Improvement* is warm, but it is also practical. Dayle offers viable tips on how to actually achieve a better life."

— Rodney Shaw,
editor of Texas District's *Sentinel*,
author of *Facets of Faith* and *People of Promise*,
associate pastor, New Life UPC, Austin, Texas

"Dayle Allen Shockley continues to be one of my favorite authors. The wonderful thing about *Home Improvement* is that it teaches you how to know God in a more intimate way. It's as if Dayle is inviting you over for a special visit with the Master. She pulls up a chair just for you, introduces you to Him, then shows you how to know Him more deeply. I felt loved after reading this book."

— **Linda Evans Shepherd,**
author, speaker,
founder of Winning Women,
Advanced Writers and Speakers Association (AWSA),
and Right to the Heart Radio

"I love the concept of this book! It is what I base my entire ministry around: living life abundantly. In *Home Improvement*, Dayle offers nine scriptural steps—wrapped in warm stories—that will help you make your life better than you ever dreamed possible!"

— **Marita Littauer,**
president, CLASServices, Inc.,
speaker, author of *You've Got What it Takes*
and *Love Extravagantly*

To my daughter Anna

*The joy you have brought to me cannot
be measured or spoken*

contents

acknowledgements

In 1995, Sharon Benson asked me to speak at the Ladies United conference in Euless, Texas. I am deeply grateful for her generous invitation. Little did I know that the subject from which I spoke that Saturday in September would lead to the writing of this book.

I will always owe a debt of gratitude to my dear parents, Rev. and Mrs. A. L. Allen. Their faith in God, their commitment to each other, and their unconditional love for me provided a solid foundation on which to build my life—a foundation that has stood the test of time.

I can't think of two greater friends than my sisters, Elaine and Gayle. Having them beside me through the years has been one of life's greatest blessings.

My undying love and appreciation goes to my husband, Stan. For every meal he prepared, for every load of laundry he washed so that I could complete this project, I will be forever grateful.

And most of all, I am thankful to God, who has dealt bountifully with me. My heart overflows with thanksgiving.

introduction

Many people live defeated and discouraged lives. They stumble through their days, burdened with fears, past hurts, unhealthy relationships, overloaded calendars, and a sour attitude to boot. Such an existence is not God's will, but is the direct work of the enemy.

Jesus said, "The thief cometh not, but for to steal, and to kill, and to destroy: I am come that they might have life, and that they might have it more abundantly" (John 10:10). Jesus came in order for every believer to have a rich and joyful life. At first glance, that may sound like a guarantee to happiness and fulfillment. It is not; it does not come to us on a silver platter; it requires our effort.

Imagine driving a car and never having the oil changed; living in a fine home and never taking out the garbage; being married and never talking to your spouse. Just as cars and homes and marriages require upkeep in order to yield satisfaction, so do our spiritual lives.

I wish I could say that I am the spiritual expert who is going to tell you everything you need to know about Christian living. And I wish I could tell you that I've never made mistakes, that I have always experienced a joyful life, walking on the straight and narrow path, never veering left nor right.

The truth is that there have been many times when I have fallen flat on my face. Times when I had to drop to my knees and beg for God's mercy. Times when it felt as if my life was spinning perilously out of control. But the good news is that, through it all, I have met some extraordinary people and have learned some amazing lessons about living. I'm still in the learning process, but I hope you'll allow me to open my heart and share with you some of the lessons I've learned thus far.

It would be unreasonable to say that the steps in this book are the exclusive way to living a joyful life. There are many things we can do to help us enjoy the full life God wants us to have. But in the chapters that follow, I have laid out nine steps that I believe can play a major role in turning defeated lives into victorious ones.

That is not to say it will be a simple 1-2-3 process. Changing your way of thinking is seldom easy. Modifying your behavior takes time and patience. But if you will dedicate yourself to learning these steps, I'm convinced you will start living a more productive and joyful life, experiencing the life Jesus desires for you to have.

step 1 | put out the welcome mat—
opening the door to God

> *Behold, I stand at the door, and knock.*
> *— Revelation 3:20*

We all have turning points in life—some pivotal moment in which the direction of our life is forever altered. These events are often tragic events: the death of a child; the illness of a spouse; the loss of a parent; the ending of a marriage.

In shattering moments like these, there is a troubling of our souls when God knocks at the door of our hearts, calling us to come closer to Him. That is not to say that God brings these events upon us, but He *uses* them as an opportunity to beckon us out into deeper waters, to experience a relationship with Him yet unknown.

It is important to note, however, that God does not only knock on our heart's door during our difficult times; He knocks at all times. There is never a moment when He isn't calling to us. He desires to turn our ordinary moments into spiritual awakenings. We get out of bed each morning to a fresh sunrise. We watch a child at play. A friend calls just to talk. All of these moments are filled with opportunities to see and hear God, but He does not impose Himself upon us. That is not His way. It is up to us to see and hear Him within these events.

Still, there are those times when we seem to listen with a greater intensity, times when we know, without a doubt, that God is knocking on our heart's door. And if we open the door to His call, it will usher us into a deeper experience with Him, bringing an extra "layer" to our lives.

I was raised in a pastor's home, going to church every time the doors opened. And I always believed I had a close relationship with God. But through the years, something happened. I guess you could say that walking with God became "old hat." I went through the motions, prayed the same tired prayers, never realizing how stale I had become.

One day, years later, I heard the knock of God in a most distinct way. I recall this day in my first book, *Whispers From Heaven*. I retell part of it here because it was that pivotal moment when I opened the door and found myself on a personal journey toward God.

Hearing the Knock at the Door

It was Valentine's Day. My husband had a rare day off, but I was not so fortunate. For two weeks my job had been grueling. An urgent project often found me putting in eleven- and twelve-hour days. So when the florist delivered a grand arrangement of a dozen red roses shortly after noon, my mood lifted. I opened the envelope and drew out the card. *Love always, Stan*, it read.

How sweet, I thought, placing the large vase of flowers on my desk. The sight of the roses cheered me and filled me with anticipation for the evening. With our daughter visiting her grandparents, it would be just the two of us—something that hadn't happened in a long while.

At 3:30, the phone rang. "Are you leaving at four?" Stan wanted to know.

"On the dot," I assured him.

"Good," he said. "I've got steaks on the grill."

The sun was softening as I drove home, one hand steadying the vase of flowers beside me. So lovely was their fragrance, I found myself relaxing. Just around the bend, a man who loved me waited.

As I drove in the garage, I glimpsed Stan out on the deck beside the smoking grill. He greeted me at the gate with a kiss. "Are you hungry?"

"Starving," I said, realizing I was. With an arm around my shoulders, he led me and the roses into the house where I couldn't believe my eyes. The dining room—normally reserved for special occasions—resembled an intimate restaurant. Glass and silver dishes sparkled beneath the warm glow of two slender, red candles. Cloth napkins lay perfectly folded beside two china plates. On my plate lay an envelope that said, "To my sweetheart." Somewhere I heard the soft strains of Jackie Gleason's orchestra.

"It's beautiful," I gasped, placing the roses in the center of the impressive table.

What followed was a luscious four-course meal, all prepared by the loving hands of my sweetheart. As the candles burned lower, I felt all of the day's tension melt away.

Dining with my husband, just being near him, hearing his voice, feeling his touch, tasting his food, filled me with a powerful longing and love for him and, at the same time, a profound knowledge of his love for me.

It wasn't a new feeling, but one often ignored because of the hectic schedules we both lived by. As the soft romantic music spilled into the little room, I knew I would remember this Valentine's Day forever.

Driving to work the next morning, I thought about the evening I'd just spent with my husband. And I sensed the Lord whisper, *That's how I want it to be between us.*

"What, Lord?" I asked, unsure what He meant. "A dozen roses? A table bathed in candlelight and spread with good food? Love notes? An evening of intimate conversation?"

Yes, He said. *Every day I send you flowers, but you seldom notice. You have a book filled with My love letters, but weeks pass without you reading them. I prepare a table just for you and Me. And I wait for you. Yet some days you never even speak to Me.*

A shiver ran up my spine as His words touched the secret places of my heart. I wanted to stop the car and weep. How foolish I had been, often dismissing the gentle wooing of God. In my busy world of deadlines and demands, how many times had I left Him dining alone like a jilted lover? Suddenly, on a busy toll road overflowing with commuters, I had an insatiable thirst for God, for a more intimate relationship with Him.

Opening the Door

As I prepared for bed that evening, I prayed, "Lord, I'm thirsty for You. I want to make You a part of my daily life, not just someone I talk to at mealtimes and a few scattered moments during the week, but I want to commune with You as a friend. Show me how."

I reached for my Bible and read: "For in him we live, and move, and have our being" (Acts 17:27-28). I liked that—knowing that in God I *lived* and *moved*. That meant that no matter where I was, God was with me.

The next morning, I cracked the blinds in my bedroom window, catching a glimpse of the peach and white impatiens I'd spent hours planting around the small rock waterfall in my backyard. The results were breathtaking. Suddenly I recalled my conversation with God on the toll road. *Flowers. Those were His flowers.* They moved so gracefully, sparkling with morning's dew drops. I knew it was my cue. "Thank You, Lord, for such incredible flowers," I said. "You are truly amazing."

I thought of all the mornings I had opened the blinds, seen the same glorious sight, and never said a simple, "Thank you." How that must have hurt the heart of God. The thought filled me with shame. "God," I said, "I'm sorry for the many mornings I've ignored You, for the countless times I've not uttered a simple prayer of thanksgiving for being allowed to see such a fantastic sight. Please forgive me."

On the drive to work the sun was radiant, slowly climbing in the morning sky. I wanted to continue my conversation with God, but didn't want to recite the same old prayers I had often offered up. And then I had an idea. I was driving down the road, literally, so why couldn't I spiritualize this activity? "Lord," I said, "steer me in the right direction today. Let me be on the path that You've designed for me."

When I got to work, I prayed again. "God, I don't just want to work for monetary gain today, but help me to also be doing Your work, seeking for that hungry soul."

The more I prayed while performing everyday activities, the more I knew God was answering my prayer from the night before; He was *showing* me how to know Him in a personal way. My daily activities could serve as launching pads for my prayers. Each task I undertook could trigger conversations with God. He wanted to be a part of the most common moments of my life. It seemed God was saying, *Open the door, My child. Let Me be your dearest friend.*

Friends. I cherished the thought.

One Saturday I decided to study some of the major characters in the Bible. What kind of relationships did they have with God? In doing so, I discovered that from Genesis to Revelation, God remained a personal God, full of patience and compassion.

God talked with Adam in the "cool of the day" (Genesis 3:8). He called Abraham his "friend" (Isaiah 41:8; James 2:23). Probably the most profound—and my favorite—story of just how personal God is can be found in the incredible story of Moses.

Here's a man who had just spent days on a mountain communing with God. Then he was handed tables of stone, written with the very "finger of God" (Exodus 31:18). Twenty-four hours later, Moses angrily threw the tablets to the ground, breaking them. Yet two chapters later, the Lord spoke to Moses "face to face, as a man speaks to his friend" (Exodus 33:11, *NKJV*). God even agreed to write the words again on a fresh pair of stones. What a Friend!

Being friends with God doesn't lessen God's holiness

21

or make it unnecessary to fear and obey Him. (Consider that Abraham was called a friend of God [II Chronicles 20:7], but in obedience to God, he would have offered his son as a sacrifice to God had an angel not stopped him.) Friendship with God does not change Him; it changes us. And so in my life, my friendship with God would ultimately change *me*. There was no way I could walk with God and not become more like Him in my spirit and attitude.

As the next few weeks unfolded, so did my awareness of God. It consumed me like a great fire, burning away the scales that had blinded me to His true nature. God had been there all the time, wanting to be with me on an intimate level, to have conversations with me throughout the day, to be a part of my real world. I was the one who had kept Him waiting, day after day, behind a closed door.

In his book *The Practice of the Presence of God*, Brother Lawrence wrote that in order to acquire a spiritual life, we must "try to converse with God in little ways while we do our work; not trying to recite previously formed thoughts." Rather, he said, we should simply "reveal our hearts as the words come to us."

In my pilgrimage toward God, I uncovered scriptures like Psalm 34:15: "The eyes of the LORD are upon the righteous, and his ears are open unto their cry." This meant He'd meet me at the kitchen table over morning coffee or talk with me on the back porch in the summer's twilight hours. I read Hebrews 4:15-16: "For we have not an high priest which cannot be touched with the feeling of our infirmities. . . . Let us therefore come boldly unto the throne of grace, that we may obtain mercy, and find grace to help in time of need."

You see, the depth of our relationship with God does not rest on God's shoulders—He is ever present and unchanging. It rests on our shoulders.

When Jesus wept over Jerusalem, He said, "I wanted to gather your children together, as a hen gathers her chicks under her wings, but you were not willing!"

"You" were not willing. God never separates Himself from us; we are the ones who separate ourselves from Him. He will be as personal, or as impersonal, as we make Him. When we find ourselves away from God, it is not God who has turned aside.

Lined along the bench beneath my bay window, sits a lively assortment of plants. Every morning, as the sun peeks over the treetops, they are flooded with yellow light. One day I discovered that the plant's leaves no longer faced the room, but had turned toward the window, searching for the sun. Instinctively, they reach for the light—even on cold, rainy days. Unless I keep them rotated, the back side of the plants will languish.

Like the plants seeking out the light in the window, I must also keep turning toward God. Annie Dillard wrote in her book *Pilgrim at Tinker Creek*, "I cannot cause light. The most I can do is try and put myself in the path of its beam."

In the Bible's final book, we hear God's gentle invitation: "Behold, I stand at the door, and knock: if any man hear my voice, and open the door, I will come in to him, and will sup with him, and he with me" (Revelation 3:20).

What an invitation! In His infinite wisdom, God grants us the freedom to choose whether or not to open the door, whether or not we will dine with Him, whether or not to walk in His light.

Many people spend a lifetime wanting a closer walk with God, never realizing that the secret lies in how wide we are willing to open the door to His presence. How much of your life are you willing to share with your Creator?

God doesn't desire for us to open the church doors for Him. Rather, He wants us to invite Him into our kitchens, into our living rooms, to find Him when we're down on Main Street or out on the lake fishing. God wants to be with us in our most mundane moments of life. He wants the door of our hearts to remain fully open to His presence at all times.

Do you hear a gentle knocking at your heart's door today? It is the lover of your soul, patiently waiting for you to welcome Him in, hoping that you desire to be with Him as much as He desires to be with you.

Ideas to help you keep the door of your heart open to God:

Start incorporating your prayers into your daily activities:

- While you're driving around town, pray, "Lord, be my guide today. Steer me in the right direction. Don't let me stray from the path You've designed for me. Keep me on the right road, dear God."
- When you're taking a shower: "Lord, create in me

a clean heart and a right spirit. Cleanse me from all unrighteousness. Wash away my evil thoughts, Lord."

- If you're ironing: "God, I want my garment to be without spot or wrinkle. I want to be clothed with Your righteousness, Lord. Help me put off my self-righteous garments, for they are as filthy rags before You."

- Maybe you're spring cleaning. "Lord, remove the cobwebs from my soul. Help me uncover any hidden sin that might be weighing me down. Search the darkest corners of my heart."

- You like to work in the yard? "Lord, let me grow according to Your plan. Help me keep the weeds of worldliness from choking out the fruit of the Spirit. Prune me, Lord, so that I will not become undisciplined in my life."

- When you're cooking dinner: "God, I thank You for the food I'm preparing. But more than that, Lord, thank You for Your Word. Help me to consume Your Word as heartily as I consume the food on my table."

Summary

Unless we keep the door of our hearts always open to God, nothing we accomplish in life will ever bring us true satisfaction. Instead, we will rush here and there, restless, reaching for more *things* to fill the void inside. Opening the door to God's presence is the first and most important step in living a joyful life. Unless you are willing to make that step, reading the rest of this book will be in vain.

step 2 | wash the windows— keeping a cheerful attitude

This is the day which the LORD hath made;
we will rejoice and be glad in it.
— Psalm 118:24

One morning on my way to the kitchen to make cof-fee, I stopped in the living room to straighten the sofa pil-lows, when something caught my eye.

It just so happens that the morning sun streams through a large bay window overlooking my backyard, and this morning there was plenty to see. The window-panes were absolutely filthy. Dumbfounded, I just stood there frozen, in a bit of shock perhaps. Why—the whole world looked utterly bleak!

Did you know that our attitude colors our world? If our attitude is dreary, our whole world will appear dreary.

What is a typical day at your house like? Do you con-stantly criticize your children for being too slow, too messy, too stubborn, too lazy, too whatever? Do you snap at everyone, including the dog?

Is your outlook on life slanted toward the negative instead of the positive? When things are going well, do you expect the bottom to fall out at any moment? When people ask how you're doing, do you immediately launch into a speech about your persistent stomachache or how the devil's been after you all day? If plans do not come off exactly as anticipated, are you unbearable to be around?

If you answered yes to more than one of the above questions, you may be suffering from a bad case of what I call the "mullygrubs." People who have the mullygrubs are always down in the dumps, always whining, always moaning, always frowning, always blaming others for their trials and tribulations, always imposing their sob stories on anyone who will listen, and always bellyaching because nobody wants to hang out with them.

If that unflattering description fits you, dear friend, I have very good news: There is a cure for the mullygrubs. But be forewarned. While the cure sounds simple enough, it may be one of the most difficult things you have ever done, and it requires the patient's complete cooperation. I'll get to the cure later; but first, let's take a look at some of the causes of this repulsive disorder.

Possible Causes of the Mullygrubs

What are some of the reasons people have the mullygrubs? Coming from a long line of grouches could be a factor; negative parents often beget negative children. Enduring tragedies or devastating setbacks at one time or another can also be a factor. There are even those who declare they were born with a negative attitude, although I do not believe that is ever the case.

Taking all of that into consideration, I believe the main reason people come down with the mullygrubs is because of their habitual negative talk. It was Isaac Singer who said, "If you keep on saying things are going to be bad, you have a good chance of being a prophet."

Complaining, whining, moaning—all of these are done through our words. And if you're like me, one complaint usually leads to another, and to another, and to another. It doesn't take long until you have spent the

29

entire day in a negative frame of mind.

In all of the research I plowed through for this chapter, most behavioral experts say that even the worst cases of the mullygrubs (actually, they don't use that exact term) can be cured, if those afflicted are willing to learn some habits of positive people.

Here are a few of them:

- Don't let trouble surprise you or overwhelm you, but learn to anticipate trouble.
- Appreciate and accept partial solutions to problems.
- List the things you value in life, then imagine them all being taken away.
- Practice cheerfulness.
- Pray for someone other than yourself.
- Be flexible.
- Regularly do something for another person.
- Share the good in your life with someone.
- Plan times of rest and relaxation.
- Sing often (even if you can't carry a tune).
- Accept what cannot be changed.
- Find the silver lining.

I have always loved the story Norman Vincent Peale shared, in one of his many books, about ferrying across the Hudson River with his mother on a foggy winter morning. As other commuters griped and whined about the weather, his elderly mother, seemingly content, said, "Norman, isn't the fog beautiful? There's something so soft and luxuriant about the way it caresses the buildings and the trees and casts them in a soft hue."

Norman looked and, sure enough, the fog was just as she described it. "All of us commuters had chosen to focus on the negative aspects of the weather," Peale wrote. "My mother found the good in it."

At my grandfather's memorial service, I listened as friends and family described him in glowing terms. He was always cheerful, they said, and never had a harsh word for anyone. And they were right. Ray Kynerd was indeed a man with admirable and desirable qualities.

I wonder what people will say about me after I'm gone. Will they be able to say kind words from their heart, or will they have to fudge the truth a little? Will they remember me as a grouch or as someone who always had a smile? Will they remember me as one who rolled with the punches of life or as someone who could never deal with adversity? Will my presence be sorely missed, or will a giant sigh of relief go up because my grating voice will no longer be heard in the neighborhood?

Some of you may be thinking, "How can I be happy with all of my problems?"

Happiness vs. Cheerfulness

Did you know that being cheerful has nothing to do with being happy? It has nothing to do with having problems or not having problems. In fact, I don't know anyone who doesn't have problems. But I do know there are those who remain cheerful *in spite of* their problems. Notice I didn't say they remain *happy* in spite of their problems. I said they remain *cheerful.*

There are many times in our lives when we cannot—and should not—be happy with our circumstances. Vehicles break down. Children get sick. Money is tight. The neighbor runs over our dog. These things do not make us happy. And nowhere in Scripture can you find where it says, "Be thou happy at all times."

But what you *can* find are scriptures that admonish us to be content in whatever circumstances we find ourselves, to run the race with patience, to be kind to one another, to endure hardness as a good soldier, to live peaceably, to return good for evil, and to bring negative thoughts into captivity. I could go on, but by now you have the general idea: our circumstances should not determine our attitudes.

If anyone has ever had a reason to be disgruntled, it was the apostle Paul. In his second letter to the Corinthians, he reported receiving a total of 195 stripes from the Jewish leaders. Three times he was beaten with rods. Once he was stoned. Three times he suffered shipwreck.

In his travels, he was often in danger from robbers, in danger from his own countrymen, in danger from the Gentiles, in danger in the city, in danger in the country, in danger at sea, and in danger from false brethren. He often went without sleep, endured hunger, suffered from cold and the lack of proper clothing.

And if all of that wasn't enough, Paul said he faced daily pressure because he was always concerned for the well-being of the churches. (See II Corinthians 11:24-33.) Yet with all of the suffering in Paul's life, he managed to sing while in prison! And it was while sitting in a jail cell, awaiting his own execution, that he managed to write remarkable letters of hope and encouragement to others.

Consider the marvelous words of Philippians 4:8: "Finally, brethren, whatsoever things are true, whatsoever things are honest, whatsoever things are just, whatsoever things are pure, whatsoever things are lovely, whatsoever things are of good report; if there be any virtue, and if there be any praise, think on these things."

I think Paul had discovered a great secret: A cheerful attitude requires mind control.

We have no control over many of the trials that come our way, and some of us have endured excruciating hardships and losses. And I do not, in any way, mean to diminish your pain or to insinuate that you should feel "no pain." Neither do I want to advocate that you should deny honest feelings, putting on happy faces and pretending that all is well, to the point of becoming insincere and artificial.

Alan Loy McGinnis, best-selling author and director of the Counseling Center in Glendale, California, reminds us that "tears are often a gift from God, and sadness is a healthy emotion." We should allow ourselves to experience these emotions to the fullest, but we should also remain optimistic that "this, too, shall pass."

I understand that it is easy to write or speak words that tend to oversimplify tough situations. I don't want to be guilty of that. However, I do believe—and Scripture backs me up—that we *can* control the things we allow our minds to dwell upon. And we *can* choose how we respond to each situation, no matter how difficult that situation may be.

Choosing to Be Cheerful

The word "cheerful" actually means, "full of good spirits."

Does that mean I can be cheerful even when I have a flat tire? Can I really be in good spirits when my car overheats in rush hour traffic?

Let me tell you about my friend Susan. In all of the years I have known her, I have never seen her when she wasn't cheerful. Even when she was having the worst day of her life, she managed to be cheerful about it.

One of the fondest memories I have of Susan occurred several years ago after a group of us had gone out to eat after church on a bitterly cold Sunday night. After we were through eating, we all scattered out in the parking lot, where Susan discovered her keys were locked inside her car—her dent-mobile, as she called it, and with very good reason; there was hardly a square inch that didn't have a dent on it.

So there she was, wondering how on earth she would get in the car. After confiscating a coat hanger from the eatery, several of the men started fishing through the window, hoping to get it done in a hurry. But the way the car's locks were made, the prospect appeared unpromising.

As each attempt failed, I watched Susan, flouncing around smiling, patting everyone on the back, saying encouraging things like, "Uncle Prentis, you are doing such a wonderful job! Dave, would you like for me to get you a cup of coffee?"

Now, it was about 40° outside, which is cold for Texans, and even though it was after eleven o'clock at night, and even though she had to catch a carpool before daylight, not once did I see that smile leave Susan's face.

Do you want to guess where I was during this whole ordeal? (This is quite embarrassing.) I was sitting in the car, grumbling about freezing to death, and wishing my husband would leave the job to the rest of the guys so I could go home.

Isn't that awful?

Before long, Susan found me. Hopping into the car, she smiled that adorable smile of hers and said, "Oh, Dayle! How do I manage to do such stupid things?" And then, she actually burst out laughing. I didn't know whether to shake her or hug her.

I don't recall how Susan's car was finally unlocked— it seems the men's persistence paid off—but I do recall that as she wheeled out of the parking lot, she left waving, smiling, and honking, being her typical, cheerful self.

Susan is proof that we can be cheerful during a small crisis like locking our keys in a car. But what about during the darkest, deepest valleys of our lives? Is it possible to remain cheerful?

In 1971, *Time* magazine published a moving profile on the famous opera star Beverly Sills. When Sills's first child was about two years old, it was discovered that the girl was almost totally deaf. Sills, so devoted to her music, was despondent to learn this, to know that her daughter would never hear the sound of her mother's voice.

To make matters worse, shortly after this discovery,

Sills gave birth to a second child, a son who was autistic. Trying to come to terms with this double tragedy, the opera star took a year off in order to regain her balance and to get her daughter enrolled in a school for the deaf. When asked if she was happy, Sills said, "I'm cheerful. There's a difference. A cheerful woman has cares but has learned how to deal with them."

Proverbs 17:22 is a familiar scripture. The New International Version reads like this: "A cheerful heart is good medicine." Maybe that's why some of us are so full of aches and pains; we aren't taking our medicine regularly. We don't have a cheerful heart. Maybe we'd feel a lot better, both emotionally and physically, if we practiced being cheerful. Ridiculous, you say?

In the late 1800s, William James was the dean of American psychologists. He was also plagued with serious bouts of despondency. After years of studying his various actions and reactions, he came to a conclusion: "By regulating [our] action," he wrote in 1892, "we can indirectly regulate [our] feeling. If our spontaneous cheerfulness be lost, we should sit up cheerfully and act and speak as if cheerfulness were already there."

While speaking at a ladies' conference several years ago, I told a story that Alan Loy McGinnis describes in his book *The Power of Optimism*. McGinnis once attended a workshop where the instructor had the group stand, put their hands high in the air, and jump up and down. Then, as they were jumping, they were told to repeat something like, "I feel terrible! I'm in a bad mood!" The participants found this "almost impossible to do." It seemed that they either had to stop the jumping motion in order to say the words or they had to stop saying the words in order to remain jumping.

After I shared this story, I coaxed my audience into trying this ridiculous exercise with me. And what happened next was rather wonderful. As soon as our feet left the ground, and even before we uttered one word, a wave of laughter swept across the building. The more we jumped, the more we laughed—all the while trying to say, "I feel terrible! I'm in a bad mood!"

I don't think our results were typical of the workshop attendees, and I worried I might never rein my audience in again, but we were left feeling quite invigorated and refreshed, which was, after all, the whole point.

If you're having a bad day, why don't you get up and try it? I guarantee you will feel better afterwards.

Curing the Mullygrubs

Do you want to end up with a headstone that says, "She never, ever found the silver lining—God rest her soul"? Of course you don't.

The good news is you don't have to. If you are willing to stop blaming your sour attitude on other people, if you are willing to spend time and effort on changing your behavior, you can cure yourself of the mullygrubs. It may be slow going, even a little painful, but in the end, it will be worth it. You will feel so much better, and your family and friends will thank you.

Are you ready? Take a deep breath and repeat after me—out loud, please:

- Hi, my name is (fill in the blank), and I am a full-fledged, bona fide grumbler.
- I am solely responsible for my irritating behavior. Not my spouse. Not my children. Not my mother. Not my father. Not my circumstances.
- I have chosen to allow other people's behavior and life's annoying situations to dictate my mood and my reactions.
- I have chosen to speak the words I speak and the tone of voice in which I speak them.
- Therefore, I can choose to stop allowing other people's behavior and life's annoying situations to dictate my mood and my reactions.
- I can choose to speak with a gentle and cheerful voice, even if I think it might kill me.
- I can choose to speak positive and uplifting words to my family, friends, and strangers.
- I can do *all* things through Christ.
- I will start today.

Summary

You may have a bay window overlooking a garden filled with exquisite roses, but if the windows are dirty, the splendor of the roses is lost. And so it is with us. If the windows of our soul are streaked with a sour attitude, the world around us will lose its beauty. And, in turn, we will lose our attractiveness to the world as well. "Life is not the way it's supposed to be," wrote Virginia Satir. "It's the way it is. The way you cope with it is what makes the difference."

step 3 | clear out the clutter—
ridding ourselves of extra baggage

> *Be renewed in the spirit of your mind.*
> *— Ephesians 4:23*

Day after day, we open closet doors and vow that one day—and soon—we are going to do some purging. But how often do we close the door, totally overwhelmed by what resides there?

The more I thought about this chapter on clutter, the more I felt a need to look at this subject from both a spiritual perspective and a literal perspective. Very few things can zap your energy like a cluttered home. I believe that until you find some method for maintaining and storing things, your life will be one of complete chaos. Not only will you suffer mentally, it can bleed over into your spiritual life as well.

Literal Clutter

As I write this, I am in the process of collecting yard sale items for a friend. The yard sale is two weeks away, but I'm not sure I will live that long; the clutter is driving me bonkers. Daily, I find myself feeling:

- distracted
- out of control
- pessimistic
- frustrated
- lethargic

Clutter brings chaos. It's that simple. I have always thought that life is much easier if there is a place for everything and everything is put back in its place.

I'm not a clutter bug. However, it is important to say that I *am* a saver of things. And I'm here to tell you that it is possible to save things without being disorganized and out of control. I say this not to boast. There are many times when I fall off the organization wagon, but the secret is not to let the clutter get out of hand before you climb back on the wagon.

A clutter bug is someone who saves too many things, and has no rhyme, no reason and no designated place for any of it. Intriguing piles accumulate in every available square inch. You may open a dresser drawer and discover one belt, two scarves, three paperback books, four bobby pins, a pack of mints, a headband, a pocketknife, and a dozen ink pens, most of which have no ink. No order. No rhyme. No reason. Just clutter.

The universe is a testament to the fact that God is a God of order. Take a look at the seasons. Each season brings a bit of its own clutter to the world. In winter, there is snow. In spring, there is pollen. In summer, there are weeds. In fall there are dead leaves.

Yet if you look closely, you will see that the coming season has a way of cleaning up the clutter left behind by the season before it. It is God's divine nature to be clutter-free, to have order.

In our natural lives, seasons come and go as well. And there are things that we hold on to: letters and cards from friends and family, clothes we no longer wear, schoolwork from our little ones. But there should come a time when we sort through these things, keeping those

41

items we are still emotionally attached to—or those things that might have future value—then letting go of the things that have run their course.

Sorting it all out

There is no standard for keeping things. What's important to your family history, or those items you feel emotionally attached to, may not be the same for me. For some reason, I have never been able to part with my daughter's shoes, dating from birth to about five years of age. She is a teenager now, and I have accepted the fact that I will probably never be able to part with these shoes. I am still attached to them. So for the time being, they rest neatly in the attic in a durable plastic tub.

In fact, if you peek inside my attic, you will find that I have acquired quite an impressive collection of boxes and plastic tubs—all holding my treasures of yesterday. But by the same token, there are hundreds of items that—through the years—I have given to charity, sold at yard sales, or thrown out because there was not room for it all. I had to force myself to decide what to keep and what to save.

For the person who would be organized, purging closets is a continual process. At least once a month, I go through my things, selecting various items for the next charity pick-up. If I didn't, I would soon drown in clutter. I would feel totally out of control, miserable in all areas of my life.

At the end of this chapter, I have listed the titles of several books that you will find helpful. And when it comes to organizing, don't be afraid to call in the pros.

Whatever money you spend will be well worth the peace of mind you will gain from it.

Spiritual Clutter

Not only are we often guilty of cluttering up our homes, we have a tendency to clutter up our minds as well. Some people refer to this as "emotional baggage," but whatever name you choose, it all produces stress. And stress can make you both spiritually and physically sick. That's why we should, occasionally, do a little mind "cleansing," coming to terms with the clutter and "baggage" that we have allowed to pile up.

My experience has been that the most common form of emotional baggage consists of past mistakes.

Do you ever sit around playing the "I wish" game with yourself? I wish I had married someone else. I wish I attended another church. I wish we had never moved here. I wish I had not taken this job. I wish I had taken that other job. I wish I had raised my children better. I wish I had spent more time with my parents. I wish my spouse had not divorced me. I wish, I wish, I wish.

Dear friend, all of us have tortured ourselves with the "I wish" game. We all have past regrets. We all have blown it at one time or another. Perhaps you blew it with your personal life—indulging yourself in sinful activities and immoral lifestyles. Maybe you blew it raising your children—too strict, too harsh, too lenient, too absent, too selfish. It could be that you blew it with your marriage or with your relationship with your siblings or parents.

Whatever your past clutter consists of, it is not God's

will for you to hang on to it. I'd like you to think about the familiar words of the apostle Paul: "Therefore if any man be in Christ, he is a new creature: old things are passed away; behold, all things are become new" (II Corinthians 5:17).

Paul made it sound so simple, but the mind is a tricky thing. Have you ever been engaged in some harmless activity when, all of a sudden and out of the blue— *wham!*—a scene from your past emerges and you find yourself filled with guilt and regret all over again?

Solutions

In times like these, there are a few things you can do to stop this thought process:

- Quote a verse of Scripture out loud. (II Corinthians 5:17 is a good one.)
- Pray a simple prayer out loud: "Dear Lord, I thank You that I am not the person I used to be. I thank You that my mistakes and failures are under the blood and that my sins are forgiven. And I thank You for the hope that I have in You."
- Play worship and inspirational tapes and CDs. Nothing runs the enemy off quite like a good song of praise. I picture the devil running out of the room with his hands cupped over his ears. Music that glorifies God is, to him, like the sound of fingernails scraping across a chalkboard.

If none of these things works for you, there is a possibility that you have not made restitution where restitution should have been made. That is not to say that you haven't repented and been forgiven, but there are times when restitution should follow repentance in order to have a complete healing of the mind.

In her wonderful book *Children Are Wet Cement*, Annie Ortlund tells the following true story:

> *Only a few months ago, Ray [her husband] and I made a date with Nels [their son] and drove out into the hills overlooking Newport Beach.*
>
> *"Nels," said Ray, "I've goofed a lot as a dad. I love you very much, but I've said and done a lot of dumb things through your fifteen years. I know I've hurt and not helped lots of times, and I just want you to know that I'm sorry."*
>
> *There was a long silence. Nels didn't quite know how to respond. "Are you leading up to something?" he asked.*
>
> *"Not a thing," said Ray. "I just wanted to say that for all the times I've blundered and hurt you and done or said stupid things to you, to put you down or make life tougher for you, I really am sorry. I just wanted to apologize.*
>
> *I chimed in from the back seat of the car: "Nels, we didn't do dumb things on purpose, but we know we've been far from ideal parents. We've blown our tempers; we've misjudged you; we haven't always handled you wisely—and that's been tough on you. We get intense and overzealous, overpicky on some issues, and we completely overlook other*

issues. We're just plain ol' dumb human beings. But our goofs have an influence on how you turn out—that's the scary part."

Ray said, "We think you're just turning out great. But whatever scars you've got, they're our fault, not yours. And don't think we don't realize that."

"That's okay," said Nels. "I think you're great."

"We sure are crazy about you, Nels," I said.

"We're so proud of you," Ray added. "You're terrific—in spite of us."

"You're great parents," said Nels.

Over the seats of the car there were pats and smiles and squeezes. That was it—and pretty soon we drove down the hill and home again.

Admitting your faults is not the easiest thing to do. It takes real men and women to say, "I was wrong. I'm sorry." But it is scriptural (James 5:16) and can be the secret to letting go of past mistakes, once and for all.

Why not take a few minutes and ask yourself if there are people in the past that you have offended. Consider the sobering words of Jesus in Mark 9:42: "And whosoever shall offend one of these little ones that believe in me, it is better for him that a millstone were hanged about his neck, and he were cast into the sea."

Are you guilty of offending someone with your actions or with your words? Perhaps there is a son or a daughter you need to have a talk with. Maybe it is a spouse or a former spouse to whom you caused irreparable damage. It could be a parent or a friend.

The best thing you can do for yourself is to stop avoiding the issue and admit your guilt. Go to the person you have wounded and confess. You might be surprised at what God will do in your life. There is a healing that comes when we humble ourselves and confess our faults one to another.

Something else that I have discovered helpful when trying to sort through the spiritual clutter in my personal life is surrounding myself with complete silence. Why is it that so many people are uncomfortable with silence these days? Is it just me, or have you noticed? It seems to me we would welcome quiet.

Consider an ordinary day. Most mornings begin with a burst of noise from the alarm clock. Breakfast is eaten between patches of conversations with family members. We may catch the news on the drive to work, or we may ride noisy buses, trains, or subways. We will spend the next eight or nine hours in a workplace saturated with words and humming machines. Our trip home often finds us listening to our favorite radio station. Once home, we bark orders to whomever will listen, and, more times than not, our dinner is devoured amidst a background of racket.

If all that is not enough, everybody from restaurant owners to dentists are bombarding us with piped-in music or big-screen TVs. Recently, I complained to a restaurant manager that the average family has little enough time to dine in peace at home. We visit restaurants to eat, I told him, not to attend a concert and not to watch television. Even some post offices now have televisions so customers can be "entertained" while waiting in line.

We tote around cell phones, pagers, and Walkmans. We buy vehicles with built-in entertainment centers, so the kiddies will have something to do on long trips.

In the clutter and clamor of our daily lives, it is easy to lose sight of who we are and what we believe. Our principles are often based solely on what we have heard from voices around us.

We need silence. In silence we can think for ourselves, looking deeply into our souls for personal values and convictions. We can identify goals and dreams and can devise a plan for fulfilling them.

Silence also puts us in tune with the extraordinary world around us. In silence we can catch sight of those often-missed gems: strips of yellow sunlight wrapping around a porch, the elaborate pattern of a leaf, a full moon's path across a still lake, downy clouds sailing against an azure sky. It is in silence that we often hear soothing, healing sounds: the mellifluous song of a bird, a gentle wind whispering through leaves, the scampering of a squirrel up the trunk of a tree, the voice of God.

Why do we cover the silence in our world?

Perhaps we are afraid of what we might encounter in the solitude of ourselves. Past mistakes. Present miseries. Future fears. But maybe if we sought out silence now and then, we would discover solutions to our predicaments. Maybe we would find the courage to make peace with our past. Who knows?

Occasionally, I do something solely for myself. It might be strolling through a flower garden, visiting a tranquil site, or just draping my grandmother's scrap quilt around me and curling up on the couch with a hot cup of coffee. But no matter how or where I position myself, my objective during these moments is to shut out the noise around me, to utterly experience the exquisite sound of silence. And I am always amazed and inspired by what I see and hear, by the gifts that are there for the taking.

As this chapter comes to an end, I invite you to do a little soul-searching. The following questions can help you get started in your pursuit of a clutter-free existence:

- Is there someone I need to go to and confess my wrongs?
- What are the top five priorities in my life, and do my actions and activities validate as much?
- What are the things that cause me the most stress?
- What are some changes I could make or things I could give up that would lessen my stress?
- How can I carve out some quiet time for myself? (Be specific.)

Summary

Coming to terms with the clutter we have allowed to pile up in our homes and in our heads takes real courage. And sometimes it takes help from gifted men and women, trained to help those caught in such dilemmas. One thing is sure: ignoring our clutter will not make it go away. Why not take the first step today? A good way to begin is by praying what is known as the "Serenity Prayer":

God, grant me wisdom to accept the things I cannot change, courage to change the things I can, and wisdom to know the difference.

A few books that deal with organizing your homes:

12 Steps to Becoming a More Organized Woman (Hendrickson Publishers), by Lane P. Jordan

Confessions of an Organized Homemaker (Betterway Publishers), by Deniece Schofield

Good-Bye Clutter: Organize and Simplify Every Room in Your Home (Carol Publishing Group), by Susan Wright.

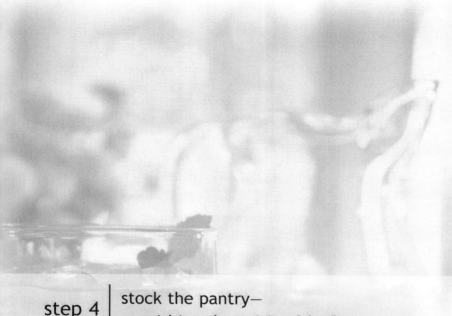

step 4 | stock the pantry—nourishing the spiritual body

*Blessed are they which do hunger and thirst
after righteousness: for they shall be filled.*
— *Matthew 5:6*

There is a void within all of us that cries out for more of God. People who do not know God often try to fill this void with drugs, sex, alcohol, money, possessions, or even with food. Emptiness consumes them, driving them to seek relief, yet they are never satisfied. Their attempts at filling the void always fall miserably short. And so they keep searching. Many of these individuals end up taking their own lives, so great is their inner hunger.

But it isn't just the sinner whose soul cries out for more of God. No matter what our relationship with God may be, there is a spiritual hunger that gnaws at us whenever we aren't as close to God as we should be. We may not recognize it as spiritual hunger, but it is there just the same.

For example, have you ever saved up to buy something special, only to discover that a few hours after you brought it home, you were wishing for yet another "something special"? Have you ever wondered what was going on? Why you still felt so miserable, when you had just purchased something you'd wanted for a long time?

I believe what we are experiencing in such moments is spiritual hunger. I believe it is God's way of saying, "No matter what you buy, it cannot completely satisfy you. Only I can fill that hunger inside."

Sadly, we often fail to recognize such gentle nudgings from the Lord. Instead of seeking out a place to pray and study during our restless or discontented moments in life, we often rush out to buy more, do more, feel more, not even aware of what propels us.

Have we become so carnally minded that we no longer recognize our own spiritual hunger?

To continually deny such hunger will ultimately result in the shriveling up of our spiritual bodies—dying of starvation, if you please. Starvation can be a long and painful process, which I will discuss later in this chapter. First, let's look at our natural bodies.

Hunger's Cycle

We may wake up in the morning, sit down to a nourishing breakfast, and eat so much that we leave the table groaning. But a few hours later, we start feeling hungry again. If that hunger is not satisfied, it will only increase with time. And if we continue ignoring our hunger, it won't be long before it drives us to the pantry, where we grab the first thing our eyes see—whether or not it is good for us. We're hungry! If Double-stuff Oreo® cookies are the only quick and easy thing in sight, then bring 'em on! Feed me! I'm starving! (Tell me I am not the only one guilty of such behavior.)

How much better it is if we take care of the physical body by feeding it properly and feeding it regularly. The stark truth is this: If we *don't* take care of our physical body by giving it proper nutrition, we will fall into that undesirable and unattractive category called "out of shape." And an unfit body often results in our becoming sickly, anemic, and weak. Many diseases are linked to poor diet.

It works exactly the same way for our spiritual bodies. Just as we can never stop feeding our natural bodies, we can never stop feeding our spiritual bodies. We fill up. We empty out. It is a perpetual cycle. There is no such thing as enough of God. Spiritual nourishment is a *daily* need for all of us.

Spiritual Starvation

I can't think of anything more tragic than to watch the process of someone dying from starvation or malnutrition. And I can't imagine what it would be like to experience a natural death because of starvation. But even more tragic is what happens when we deprive our souls of needed spiritual nutrition. As in the physical, spiritual starvation does not happen overnight, but gradually.

Whenever we turn our lives over to God, our spiritual hunger ceases; we are filled to overflowing. There is a rejoicing in our souls. Life is good. The birds are singing. The sun is shining. At last—total satisfaction within!

Wouldn't it be nice if we could maintain that incredible feeling without ever having to do another thing? Imagine waking up day in and day out to a feeling of complete inner fulfillment.

Ah, but dear friend, that's not God's plan. Just as God created our physical bodies to grow hungry if we don't feed them, He put within us a soul that can only be satisfied by regular spiritual feedings. And this is where the enemy uses his best tool called temptation.

Remember what I said earlier in this chapter about

what happens to our physical bodies if we don't feed them properly and regularly? We become sick, anemic, and weak. Now think about that for a moment as it relates to our spiritual bodies. If we fail to establish a regular "feeding" for our spiritual bodies, and if we fail to feed our spiritual bodies the proper foods, we become tempted by Satan's smorgasbord of unhealthy offerings. We will end up gorging ourselves with "double-stuff" cookies!

Perhaps you sang the song in Sunday school that said the devil is a sly old fox. Believe it. He's waiting day and night for your hunger to kick in, so he can thrust something unhealthy in front of you. And he knows precisely what flavor and brand to put in the pantry. Whatever your weakness, the enemy of your soul knows it. And that's exactly how spiritual starvation and malnutrition begin. Little by little, you find yourself exchanging proper spiritual sustenance for whatever satisfies at the moment.

Your weakened spiritual condition may begin innocently enough. What could possibly be wrong with going shopping, accepting a lucrative job, taking a vacation, or getting involved in a harmless hobby? The answer is: nothing. In and of itself, these are safe activities. But it is when we start using such activities to fill up the empty places in our lives that they become detrimental to our spiritual health.

It might surprise you, but the enemy of your soul is not nearly as interested in watching you die spiritually, as much as he is interested in watching you become sickly, anemic, and powerless. He knows that if he can keep you weak, he can deceive you into believing that things are OK. When we are filled with other things, we do not recognize our own hunger. We quickly fall into what is called a "lukewarm" state—that comfortable, but dangerous, state that Jesus talked about in Revelation 3:16.

Satan loves it when we are lukewarm. Neither hot nor cold. Neither in nor out. He knows that the man or woman who completely turns his or her back on God is a bigger threat, in some ways, because that person may one day wake up in the pigpen of life and realize, "Wait just a minute! I'm starving to death here with these pigs, while my Father has a storehouse full of nourishing food. I'm going back to the Father's house!"

The lukewarm—or spiritually weak—individual is often unaware that anything is wrong until it's too late. It is in Satan's best interest to keep you a weak believer.

Feeding the Spiritual Body

In order for the natural body to function and stay alive, it must have minerals, vitamins, proteins, starches, fats, and water. Health experts say that when one or all of these necessary things are taken away, a person will become malnourished and will eventually die.

When a man is rescued at the point of starvation, one of two things will happen. If the body cells have only been weakened, the body will respond to proper feeding and bounce back. But if the body cells have been damaged beyond repair, the body will not respond to proper feeding, and death will occur.

The same is true for the spiritual man. How often have you seen people turn away from God, only to return at some point, eager to begin anew? They were rescued in time. Their spiritual man bounces back from its malnourished state. But others turn away from God, return to God at some point, but are never again strong in their faith. What happens is their appetite for the world surpasses their appetite for God.

Scripture says that those who hunger and thirst *after righteousness* shall be filled (Matthew 5:6). I suppose we could say that another way: *Unless* we hunger and thirst after *righteousness*, we will never be filled.

Nourishing the spiritual body can be done in a number of ways, but none are so effective as:

- Studying the Bible
- Hearing the preached Word of God
- Establishing a consistent prayer life

Let's take a look at these three elements.

Studying the Bible

"Thy word is a lamp unto my feet, and a light unto my path" (Psalm 119:105).

I have a number of Bibles that I use, but my study Bible is a dark green, King James Version that my parents gave me for Christmas in 1973, the one whose pages and margins are all marked up. To be honest, it looks a mess. But whenever I find myself in the midst of a spiritual storm, the first thing I reach for is this Bible. As the Lord ministers to me through certain scriptures, I underline the verses, often scribbling the date in the margin, to boot. My attachment to this Bible is so great that I cannot imagine my life without it.

Since I have other Bibles that I carry with me to church, few people have seen my beloved, dark green Bible, but those who do often leap back in horror. How could I write in my Bible? How irreverent!

Nonsense. It is these things—the notes in my Bible and the underlined scriptures—that are often a source of strength and comfort during life's storms. Coming across marked verses and dates in the margins becomes one of those "aha" moments. *God, I know You'll get me through this storm in one piece because You got me through that hurricane in 1998. See, it's right here in the margin. Do You remember that storm, Lord? What a whopper! And just when I thought I was a goner, You threw out a lifeline for me, Lord—it was this very scripture right here that kept me afloat—the same one I have uncovered again today.*

Before long, I'm rejoicing in God's faithfulness, certain, beyond a single doubt, that I will survive the current storm and all the storms that may follow. The proof is in the margins.

I've been reading from my old green Bible for almost thirty years now, and I can echo the psalmist who said, "Thy word is a lamp unto my feet, and a light unto my path."

I encourage you to fall in love with God's Word. It is necessary for keeping your spiritual body in tip-top shape.

Hearing the Preached Word of God

"And he gave some, apostles; and some, prophets; and some, evangelists; and some, pastors and teachers; for the perfecting of the saints" (Ephesians 4:11-12).

There is nothing quite as nourishing for the spiritual body as hearing the preached Word of God from a seasoned minister. Churches should function like spiritual gas stations, where believers fill their spiritual tanks and find strength to go out and serve in their communities.

Allow me to step out on a limb for a moment. If you attend a church where the pastor does nothing but criticize and condemn the saints every time they darken the doors, you will never be a strong Christian. You simply cannot grow and flourish in a critical atmosphere. Travel to any harsh environment, and you will find desolation. Nothing grows there. It is the same with people.

Perhaps such pastors believe they can inspire you to draw closer to God by delivering abrasive messages, pointing out your lack of spirituality and making sure you know how upset they are with your shortcomings. But just as children cannot thrive under the guidance of fault-finding parents, believers cannot thrive under the leadership of fault-finding pastors.

Certainly there are times when pastors must rebuke. Paul said, "Preach the word; be instant in season, out of season; reprove, rebuke, exhort"—how?—"with all long-suffering" (II Timothy 4:2). This is the key.

I once saw a sign that said: "Jesus did not say club my sheep or shear my sheep. He did say, 'Feed my sheep.'" Find a pastor who knows how to feed the sheep, and you will grow and mature in the way God intended. You must have a preacher in your life or your spiritual body will become weak and frail.

Establishing a Consistent Prayer Life

"Pray, lest ye enter into temptation" (Luke 22:46).

Last, but by all means not least, in order for our spiritual bodies to be healthy, we must establish a regular prayer life.

When people pray, things happen. Prayer turns spiritual weaklings into spiritual giants. Nobody knows that better than Satan. And that is why he hates prayer warriors. If you want to see the devil kick into high gear, just start a daily time of prayer. Nothing stirs up his dander like a person talking seriously with God.

You see, dear friend, the enemy of your soul doesn't really mind if you pray once a week, or over meals, or while at church. As long as he can keep you from establishing a *regular* prayer life, he isn't too worried at all. He knows that during your idle moments he has plenty of time and opportunity to tempt you with a host of alluring activities that can hinder your spirituality. He understands just how *powerless* you are to resist these things without a daily time of prayer. In short, if you do not have a consistent prayer life, the devil has you within arm's reach.

So why don't we pray more?

No time, you say.

If only we viewed prayer as John Wesley when he said, "I have so much to do that I must spend several hours in prayer before I am able to do it."

Look at the inspirational writings of Frederick W. Robertson on daily prayer:

Go not, my friend, into the dangerous world

without prayer. You kneel down at night to pray, drowsiness weights down your eyelids; a hard day's work is a kind of excuse, and you shorten your prayer, and resign yourself softly to repose. The morning breaks; and it may be you rise late, and so your early devotions are not done, or are done with irregular haste.

There has been that done which cannot be undone. You have given up your prayer, and you will suffer for it.

Temptation is before you, and you are not ready to meet it. There is a guilty feeling on the soul, and you linger at a distance from God. It is no marvel if that day in which you suffer drowsiness to interfere with prayer be a day in which you shrink from duty.

Moments of prayer intruded on by sloth cannot be made up. We may get experience, but we cannot get back the rich freshness and strength which were wrapped up in those moments.

From the time I entered high school, until the day I moved away, my father's voice in prayer woke me every morning. Daddy wasn't—and isn't—a perfect man (there are none), but he has always been a praying man.

His example in prayer has taught me two things: (1) no matter how miserably you may fail God, He is waiting for you the next morning, waiting to forgive you and to strengthen you, and (2) it really is possible to have a consistent prayer life.

Even to this day, whenever my parents come to visit, I wake in the early morning hours to find my father in the dining room, having his morning prayer and devotion. I cannot tell you the impact this consistent example has had upon my life. And eternity alone will reveal just what has been accomplished because of Daddy's prayers.

Jesus left us a wonderful example, rising early to pray, making time to get alone with His heavenly Father. And His instructions regarding prayer are clear: "When you pray, go into your room, close the door and pray" (Matthew 6:6, *NIV*).

Coming together in prayer, as a church body, is all well and good, but whenever I feel an urge to be an intercessor in prayer, I want to be alone. Not always, but generally. Jesus had a reason for saying, "When you pray, go into your room, close the door and pray." Being alone with God is a sure sign of our devotion. Nobody is looking. Nobody is listening. It's just you and your Lord.

It is interesting to note that the great men of the Bible were *alone* when God did His greatest work in their lives. Remember Moses, Elisha, Elijah, Jacob, Gideon, Peter, John the Baptist, and Cornelius. And don't forget about Mary, the mother of Jesus.

Without question, regular time spent in prayer is essential in order for the spiritual body to thrive.

Some questions to ask yourself:

- How much time do I spend in prayer and Bible study every day?

- Am I faithful to the house of God?
- Are the extracurricular actives I engage in making me a more spiritual person, or are they making me more worldly?
- Am I willing to give up the activities that keep me carnally minded?
- Do I spend more time on the telephone with friends than I do on the "telephone" with God?
- Do I make time in my day for God?
- Do I have my own special place of prayer in my home?

Summary

When we try to satisfy our spiritual hunger with material things and carnal activities, we will soon find ourselves spiritually depleted. We will be no match for Satan's attacks. Why not do a little inventory in your spiritual pantry today; toss out the harmful products and stock up on those things that nourish the soul.

step 5 | take out the trash—
letting go of past hurts

Let all bitterness, and wrath, and anger, and clamour,
and evil speaking, be put away from you.
— Ephesians 5:31

Have you ever left a Styrofoam meat tray in the garbage can overnight? By sunup the next morning, the whole kitchen smells to high heaven. Your first priority is to get that offensive odor out of the house. But what if, instead of tying up the trash bag and hightailing it to the curb, you suddenly say, "I think I'll keep this open a while longer; I might need to dig around in here later on"?

You wouldn't consider doing such a ridiculous thing. You know that the longer you leave the stinky garbage bag open, and the more you dig through it, the worse it's going to smell. Garbage is garbage is garbage. The only place for it is OUT! Who in the world would want to keep stinky garbage in the kitchen for later inspection?

Well, dear friend, the kitchen is not the only place where garbage accumulates, and sometimes we're guilty of not disposing of it promptly. In fact, I'll be bold and say that some of you reading this book have a personal "garbage bag" that you have refused to tie up and dispose of. And even though it nearly takes your breath away every time you do it, you pilfer through it day after day, week after week, year after year.

Perhaps you're wondering what on earth I'm talking about. Let me explain.

Internal Garbage

Although she would deny it, my dear mother is perhaps the world's greatest counselor and has a devoted following that can be found coast-to-coast. Many years ago, after I had been dealt a severe personal insult from someone I truly loved, Mother and I sat at the kitchen table sharing one of our many late-night chats.

Though it had been months since the incident occurred, I still held on to it with both hands. My anger and hurt could be heard in every word I spoke and could be seen in every movement I made. I simply refused to give it up. It was the first thing I thought about in the morning and the last thing I remembered at night. And the more I talked about it, the more I hurt. And the madder I got. And the more I wanted to take my revenge on the offender.

But there sat my mother that night, just waiting for me to take a breath from my ranting. And when I did, she said something that, in time, totally changed me. She said, "Sweetheart, in this life you sometimes get a lot of garbage thrown at you. And whenever you do, you should visualize yourself gathering it up and putting it in a trash bag. Then, tie it up and never open it again, because if you open that bag again, it will smell worse than it did when you put it in there. You must forgive and go on."

Truer words were never spoken.

If you're old enough to read this, I am certain you've been wounded by someone at some time or another. We all have. Some of our injuries are superficial, having no real lasting effect on our lives.

- A friend borrows a few dollars and never repays you.

- Your husband decides to play golf on your anniversary.
- An associate takes the credit for the work you did.

But some of our wounds have been deep and unspeakable, changing the direction of our lives and forcing us to travel down roads we did not choose.

- A parent abuses you, physically or emotionally.
- A spouse leaves you high and dry, without a biblical or just cause.
- A friend forsakes or betrays you in your time of need.
- People you thought you could trust spread rumors about you, harming your reputation in the community.
- A daughter rebels against your teachings and becomes pregnant before marriage.
- A son is killed or disfigured by a drunk driver.

Such wounds generally require us to go through what we know as the stages of grief: shock, denial, disbelief, anger, sadness, acceptance, and, finally, healing. Most experts agree that reaching that final stage of grief can be a slow process—three to seven years, some say—and should not be rushed.

Regrettably, there are those who get stuck in the anger stage. By doing so, they often end up, unknowingly, pushing away those who would like to be there to comfort them.

When I met Christine, it didn't take me long to wish I never had. From the minute she appeared in my life, I don't think I ever heard her utter one positive syllable. She had found her husband with another woman, and that is all—and I do mean all—that Christine talked about. If I said what a glorious day it was, she said that if your husband had slept with another woman it wouldn't look so glorious.

Every waking moment of her life seemed to be saturated with thoughts of this man and the evil deed he had committed against her. It seemed she wasn't happy unless she was actively spreading her misery to those around her.

I hesitate to admit it, and I'm sorry if I sound insensitive, but before long, I began avoiding Christine. Nothing I ever said to her helped; she remained at the same point from the time we met until the last time I saw her. Christine was perfectly content to keep digging in her personal trash bag. To tie it up and dispose of it would have left her with no excuses for her miserable attitude.

A Better Way

Please don't misunderstand me. I do not mean to trivialize Christine's intense pain. Nor do I mean to say that such devastating events in life should not be talked about with other people. Quite the contrary. I believe that they *should* be talked about. I just happen to believe that there is a better way to talk about such tragic occurrences than merely spreading misery from one to another. After all, shouldn't the goal be to reach the point of healing and acceptance?

I am grateful that there are special friends we have who are always there when we need a shoulder to cry on. We can open up our souls and let our feelings out, knowing that our secrets are safe with them. And I thank God that we have pastors and pastors' wives who can offer prayer and counseling on our behalf.

But in addition to having these wonderful people in our lives during trying times, I am an enthusiastic proponent of professional Christian counseling. I know, from personal experience, that such counseling can bring with it great results and great relief.

I believe that God gives people certain gifts and abilities to help us on our journey through this world. When our teeth need fixing, we go to a dentist. When our pets get sick, we take them to a veterinarian. You wouldn't dream of taking your broken-down car to a plumber for repairs, would you?

But when our lives and marriages and families are falling apart, why do we hesitate from consulting someone who is a professional in the business? Why treat our most sacred possessions with such indifference and triviality? Yes, God has the answers to all of life's problems. In fact, he could fill our teeth, heal our pets, even repair our broken-down cars, but God uses *people*.

I know that I'm talking about a subject that often gets mixed reviews. But I dare say that those who are opposed to Christian counseling have never been inside a Christian counselor's office. They speak of things they know not of. But I speak from experience.

Proficient Christian counselors use the Word of God

as a guide in their counseling sessions. They will pray with you. In addition, they are trained to help bring you back to wholeness, whenever your world is turned upside down.

When I was in counseling many years ago, my counselor asked me to go home and write about a painful incident that had occurred years earlier. She asked me to describe, in detail, the place, time of day, the clothes I wore, the emotions that surfaced—all of it—during that distressing event.

It was an excruciating task, requiring all of the courage I could muster. I cried. I screamed. I clobbered the notepad with my fists. But when the words lay quiet in front of me, when I forced myself to write down every agonizing second, and identify every emotion that rose up in me, there came a moment of certain release.

For more than a decade, I had silently held the pain close, afraid to open my hand for a second look, lest I be overtaken with grief. If only I had known that the only way to be rid of the pain was to closely examine it, to talk about it, to write about it.

Having a Christian counselor to prompt me in this way has made an enormous impact upon my life. Since then, I've made a habit to write down encounters that wound me, and I've been amazed at the cleansing that comes from putting words to paper.

The Will to Forgive

Whether or not you seek Christian counseling during critical moments in your life, moving on, away from your disappointments, away from your hurts and tragedies, is not easy. And sometimes, forgiving seems like an impossible, if not cruel, task. Let's take a close look at what it means to forgive and why we should forgive.

"Forgiving is love's toughest work," wrote Lewis B. Smedes in his book *Forgive and Forget.* "It occurs within a storm of complex emotions."

Smedes says there is hurting, hating, healing, and a coming together, with the ultimate goal being reconciliation. However, reconciliation cannot be accomplished without deciding to forgive.

Forgiving one another is something that I believe we take all too lightly. Technically, forgiving someone is a choice. You hurt me; I can choose to forgive you, or I can choose not to forgive you. But if you study the Word of God, you'll see that to the Christian, forgiveness is not an option. It is something we *must* do.

In Matthew 6:14-15 Jesus said, "For if ye forgive men their trespasses, your heavenly Father will also forgive you: but if ye forgive not men their trespasses, neither will your Father forgive your trespasses."

This passage alone should be incentive for us to forgive those who hurt us. But there are probably some of you who have someone you need to forgive. The hurt that was dealt you is never far away from your thoughts. You talk about it at every opportunity. You lose sleep over it. You seek ways to get revenge.

In essence, you are digging through the trash. And you will never get rid of the "stench" until you are willing to forgive.

Why Forgive?

Some of you have been wounded deeply—both physically and emotionally. "Why should I forgive?" you want to know.

Aside from the fact that God commands us to forgive one another, carrying past hurts around is a self-defeating activity. It's like trying to walk with a ball and chain clamped on your ankle. It slows you down. Every time you would move forward, the ball and chain are there, reminding you of those things that were done against you and opening the wound all over again. And as long as the wound is never allowed to heal, it will always bring you pain.

Ironically, many people have the idea that by not forgiving the offender, they are getting even with the offender. Not so. You see, the ones who hurt you do not lose sleep over the fact that they hurt you. They do not have trouble eating because they hurt you. They are moving on with their lives, in spite of having destroyed yours. Ironically, refusing to forgive someone doesn't hurt the offender at all. It only hurts *you*.

It has been said that forgiveness is a gift you give yourself. And that is true. It is only when you truly forgive that the heavy ball and chain will come off, allowing you to move forward to a brand-new level in Christ.

I heard a story one time about a woman who had suffered years of physical abuse from her husband. She finally managed to break away from the hold he had on her, and even though she had remarried years later, those feelings of hate and resentment were never far away. It was like a giant stone tied to her waist; she was never free.

One day, an idea came to her. She went to the store and bought ten helium balloons and a black felt-tip marker. Then she drove out to an open field. Taking the balloons, one at a time, she wrote a number on each one, beginning with the number one, all the way to number ten.

Getting out of her car with those ten balloons, she walked out into the field and sat down. She thought of the ten years of abuse she had suffered at the hands of her ex-husband, and to her amazement, she realized that she was still suffering. So much so that it seemed only yesterday that the injuries had occurred.

Sitting there on the hard ground, she said it was like the skies opened up and, for the first time, she knew, more than ever, that she had never forgiven her former husband for the awful acts committed against her, and that it was she who had suffered because of it. She wondered why it had taken so long to realize that. This day, she determined to forgive.

And with that resolve, she released the balloons, visualizing all of the hurt, the pain, and the hatred that she had carried around for all of those years, floating away from her and out of sight.

She says it was as if a concrete block lifted off her shoulders. Suddenly, for the first time in ten years, she felt truly freed from her past.

A certain teacher once had this to say about forgiveness. "Let go. Why do you cling to pain? There is nothing you can do about the wrongs of yesterday. It is not yours to judge. Why hold on to the very thing which keeps you from hope and love?"

Release those hurts you've held on to for years. Free yourself from pain and leave judgment and vengeance to God.

Signs of Forgiveness

How will you know when you've truly forgiven another person? Here are some things to consider:

- When you can pray for the offender with a genuine compassion.
- When you are sincerely concerned about the offender's well-being.
- When you can wish them well and really mean it.

Smedes offers the following thoughts about forgiving:

- Forgiving is not ignoring, excusing, or justifying immoral or devious behavior.
- Forgiving is not taking the blame for the offender's immoral or devious behavior.
- Forgiving is not overlooking your feelings about painful events.
- Forgiving is not allowing the offender back into your life for a repeat performance; just because you forgive someone doesn't mean that you have to continue investing time and effort into a relationship.
- If reconciliation occurs between the offender and the victim, it should only be done so after *both* parties

have had an honest coming together, each bringing something to the table. The offender must bring honesty, repentance, and a promise not to repeat the past. The victim must bring forgiveness and a willingness to give the offender a fresh start.

- Even if the offender refuses to come to the table of reconciliation, forgiveness should still be given, for your own sake.

Summary

An unforgiving spirit produces sleepless nights and tormented days. It consumes you like a slow-burning fire, until finally the very embers of your life are snuffed out. The only way to experience a joyful life is by not letting the "trash" pile up around you. And the only way to get rid of the trash is by *choosing* to forgive. It is truly for your own good.

step 6 | tend to the flower beds—
growing healthy relationships

He which soweth sparingly shall reap also sparingly;
and he which soweth bountifully
shall reap also bountifully.
— II Corinthians 9:6

Spring is the time of year when the earth calls to me. I pull on a pair of gardening gloves, collect my spade and trowel, and set out to prepare my flower beds for a fresh season of growth.

Removing winter's abuse from the land is a grueling job. But to feel the cool, clean soil in my hands once again, to smell its rich aroma, to plant something in the barren earth brings with it a deep satisfaction that only gardeners understand.

As each plant goes into the ground, there is a sense of expectancy. I know that one day, if I'm patient and diligent with my garden, I'll sit out in the early evening— surrounded by a host of yellow pansies and pink impatiens—enjoying spring's promise.

It sounds simple enough, but true gardeners know just how time consuming it is to produce healthy and flourishing gardens. They know the toil that goes into it, and they understand that without consistent maintenance, the garden's loveliness would last only a few weeks—at best—before withering.

Gardens have four basic needs: *watering, feeding, weeding,* and *pruning.* If one of these needs isn't met, the garden may survive, but it will be weak and unrewarding.

This chapter is about relationships. Relationships are much like gardens. Without regular attention and maintenance they, too, will become weak and unfulfilling. It is my prayer that you will find something within these pages that will motivate you into becoming the absolute best "gardener" of your relationships that you can be. But before you begin reading, I must tell you that I'm no expert. I do not always have my act together—in any of my relationships. In fact, I fail very often, and often miserably.

But what I can offer you is personal experience. And in addition to my personal experience, I have spent much of my writing life—fifteen years now—researching and writing about relationships, consulting with those who are "experts" in the various relationships that make up our lives, and always using the Bible for the final authority on relationships.

Perhaps you're wondering why I'm discussing relationships at all. It's simple. Our lives revolve around our relationships. We have parents, siblings, spouses, children, friends, co-workers, church family and pastors. If these relationships are broken down and falling apart, it is impossible to live the abundant life God intended for us to have. We are the sum total of our relationships, and, as followers of Christ, we must maintain them.

Where to Start?

As I contemplated this chapter, I knew that there was not room to discuss all of the relationships that make up our lives, so I had to choose. Is one relationship more important than others?

I believe the answer to that question is a resounding *yes.*

When God created the world, that creation included a man and a woman who ultimately were joined together as man and wife, becoming not only the catalyst for the world's population, but also the foundation upon which every other relationship would stand.

When the marital relationship breaks down, the consequences are not only immediate, but reach into future generations as well.

Many years ago, I asked my mother a simple question: What has caused the youth of today (and that was twenty-five years ago) to be so defiant and unruly? Her answer was firm and has stayed with me all these years. "It's a breakdown in the home," Mother said.

Being young and unmarried at the time, I took her at her word. But after twenty-five years of studying human behavior and examining statistics, there is no doubt that Mother was right. If our marriages are healthy and in line with the Word of God, our children will most likely be "healthy" as well.

Ultimately, a strong marriage is the underpinning of those who will follow in our footsteps. It is the most important earthly relationship that we will ever enter into, so let's take a look at some "gardening" tips that can help make our marriages the strongest and healthiest they can be.

A Look at Personalities and Temperaments

We all have unique personalities and temperaments. Perhaps you've heard of the ever popular Type A and Type B personalities:

Type A Characteristics:
- Competitive and driven
- Impatient and often harsh
- Irritated easily (invented road rage)
- Works fast and furious
- Seeks challenges
- Performs poorly on judgment tasks
- Tends not to rise to top levels of management

Type B Characteristics:
- Calm manner
- Performs well on judgment tasks
- Work is accurate
- More high-level managers are Type B

Additionally, much ado has been made about the four "temperaments":
- The Sanguine (extrovert, talker, optimist)
- The Melancholy (introvert, thinker, pessimist)
- The Choleric (extrovert, doer, optimist)
- The Phlegmatic (introvert, watcher, pessimist)

Undoubtedly, there can be great value to understanding each other's personalities and temperaments, knowing how a spouse might respond to various actions and events. I'm certain that all of our relationships would be much more rewarding if we took the time to get to know each other's unique traits and then made sure we respected those traits in the future.

Regrettably, most of us don't take the time to examine human behavior so closely. Things happen. We react without thinking about what kind of personality and temperament someone may possess. Feelings are hurt. Spirits are crushed. And all we can say is a pathetically inadequate, "I'm sorry. Nobody's perfect, you know."

However—and that is a major however—the fact that we are imperfect human beings does not give us the right to say the first thing we think of, behaving as offensively as we desire, taking action against a spouse and offending each other. We may not give a hoot about our spouse's personalities and temperaments, but we *must* give a hoot about what the Word of God has to say about how we deal with each other.

I often hear people saying things like, "Well, God knows how I am. He made me this way and that's just the way I am. If that offends my wife or my husband, tough luck."

Listen, dear friend. That kind of attitude has destroyed many relationships. Yes, God knows how you are. Yes, God made you. But if you think your bad behavior is excused, just because "God knows how you are," you are sadly mistaken.

When we are born again, something wonderful happens: we become new creatures in Christ (II Corinthians 5:17). It is the power of the Holy Spirit working within us that gives us the strength to bring our old nature under control. (See Acts 1:8.) And whenever our old nature rears its ugly head, it's a sure sign that we are no longer walking in the Spirit.

Without question, the Word of God is forever settled. And I'm happy to report that it gives us *specific* and *precise* guidelines for living. Not only does the Bible tell us how to treat our spouse, it covers every individual with whom we have a relationship—including our enemies! Isn't that marvelous? And there is not one version of the Bible for Type A personalities and a different version for Type B personalities. Whether you're a Sanguine, Melancholy, Choleric, or Phlegmatic, in the end, we must all line up with the Word of God. It is the final directive.

Basic Needs of a Marriage

I don't think there is any doubt that God's original plan for marriage was that it last forever. In Matthew 19:6, Jesus—when speaking of marriage—said: "What therefore God hath joined together, let not man put asunder." And when the disciples questioned why Moses had authorized a "writing of divorce," Jesus went on to say that, because of the hardness of the people's hearts, Moses put up with the practice of divorce. "But from the beginning," Jesus said, "it was not so."

I understand that sometimes extenuating circumstances result in the demise of a marriage, but today half of all marriages will end in divorce, the large majority of those being for frivolous reasons.

When my husband and I first married, we attended a "young marrieds" class at church and were taught a series of extensive lessons on marriage called, "Building a Partnership." I kept my notes and handbook all these years, never realizing I would draw on them for a future book of my own. Regrettably, the handbook does not show who authored these lessons, and I have been unable to locate this study in bookstores, so I cannot give credit where it belongs. Throughout this chapter, I will be drawing from this material, and if I quote directly from the handbook, I will say as much.

The first and foremost need in a marriage is for both parties to have a strong relationship with Jesus Christ. Without that, there is little anyone can say or do to revive a failing marriage. In his book *Love for a Lifetime*, Dr. James Dobson writes, "A personal relationship with Jesus Christ is the cornerstone of marriage." Indeed!

The Family Organization

Corporations have what is called an *organizational chart* for their employees to refer to if they are ever in doubt as to who is in charge of whom. Here's what God's organizational chart for the family looks like, based on Ephesians 5:22-33 and Ephesians 6:1.

THE FAMILY

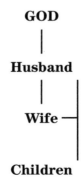

GOD

Husband

Wife

Children

Regardless of what our opinions may be about God's order for the family, it is His order, it is perfect, it is for our good, and anything other than what He designed is displeasing in His sight.

Now that we've established our organizational chart, let's take a look at the job duties.

God's Obligations

Is God obligated to us? The Bible is filled with "exceeding great and precious promises" (II Peter 1:4) that God is obligated to fulfill. However, each promise is predicated on our obedience. As long as we put God in His rightful place in our homes, and as long as we are obedient to His Word, fulfilling our obligations as outlined in the Bible, God will perform that which He has promised.

The Role and Obligations of Husbands

Ephesians 5:25-28 is crystal clear about a man's responsibility to his wife. "Husbands, love your wives," Paul wrote, "even as Christ also loved the church." But note that Paul doesn't stop there. He added, "and gave himself for it."

Why did Paul elaborate? Why wouldn't it have been enough to just say, "Husbands, love your wives, even as Christ also loved the church"? But Paul felt a need to go further by adding, "and gave himself for it."

Let's look at this extraordinary love for a moment. Christ loved the church unconditionally. Romans 5:8 says that while "we were yet sinners, Christ died for us." He didn't say, "OK, whenever you straighten up your act and start showing your love for Me, *then* I will love you and sacrifice Myself for you."

No. Christ loved the church *first*. He said, in essence, it doesn't matter what you do, or how you behave, or how you treat Me. I'm going to love you anyway. I have *chosen* to love you unconditionally, giving up My life for your redemption.

But why? Why did Christ love the church unconditionally, going so far as to hang on a cross, *while we were yet sinners*?

The enlightening answer can be found in Ephesians 5:26-27: "that he might sanctify and cleanse it with the washing of water by the word, that he might present it to himself a glorious church, not having spot, or wrinkle, or any such thing; but that it should be holy and without blemish."

You see, Jesus knew that if He chose to love us unconditionally, it would inspire us to respond to His love, willingly allowing Him to cleanse us so we could be spotless, without wrinkle, and without blemish. That would not be possible if Christ had not loved us first, *while we were yet sinners*.

It boggles the human mind that a sinless Christ would love us—rank sinners—so much that He would go to a cross. But once we saw the lengths to which Christ would go to show His unconditional love, we chose to follow Him, to worship Him, to reverence Him, to express our love to Him. Sadly, there are many who still reject Christ's love, but we who accept it, do so only because of Christ loving us first. In I John 4:19 we read: "We love him, *because* he first loved us." (Emphasis mine.)

Just as Christ's unconditional love for the church resulted in His having a glorious church, holy and without blemish to present to Himself, so is there a great reward that comes when husbands love their wives—unconditionally.

When a wife sees that she is loved by her husband— regardless of whether or not she always says and does everything by a certain method—she is blown away. In return, she will choose to follow her husband, to admire him, to reverence him, to express her love for him. Just as we feel secure knowing that Christ's love for us will never fail—no matter what—so does the wife who knows she has her husband's unconditional love.

There are scores of husbands in this country who want to "wear the pants" in the family. They want to be the "head of the house." They want to tell their wives what to do, and in no uncertain terms. They often use—even abuse—their authority over their wives. But many of them never fulfill their God-given responsibilities to their wives—to love them unconditionally. And they wonder why their wives often revolt. They wonder why their wives have trouble submitting to them and respecting them.

It goes without saying that if a man's relationship with God is strong and intact, his relationship with his wife will be strong and intact. Show me a man who claims to have a committed relationship with Jesus Christ but neglects his wife's needs, and I'll show you a man who is displeasing to God.

The Word of God is plain and sure. Ephesians 5:25

says that husbands are to love their wives "as Christ also loved the church." And, I'm sorry guys, but that love took Christ to a cruel cross. "So ought men to love their wives," Paul said.

Now I don't think Paul pictured a man literally hanging on a cross for his wife, but I do believe God intends for a husband to bear whatever cross—burdens, if you please—necessary in order to meet the needs of his wife. Sometimes it isn't easy. Sometimes it requires the greatest of sacrifices. But Christ gave up His *life* for the church. "So ought men to love their wives," Paul said.

Someone asked me one day, "If you were handicapped and couldn't care for yourself, would you expect your husband to quit his job and take care of you?"

I thought a minute, then said, "I would expect my husband to make whatever arrangements were necessary in order to see that I was taken care of. And God would expect it, too." If that means limiting his obligations, or changing jobs, or even early retirement, so be it. God wrote the rules for husbands, and they are non-negotiable. Very little is clearer in the Bible than a man's obligation to his wife.

I think it is important to digress here and take a look at the conversation Peter had with Jesus in Luke 18. Peter reminded Jesus that he and the disciples had "left all" to follow Him. And in Luke 18:29-30, Jesus responded to Peter: "Verily I say unto you, There is no man that hath left house, or parents, or brethren, or wife, or children, for the kingdom of God's sake, who shall not receive manifold more in this present time, and in the world to come life everlasting."

At first glance, this may seem contradictory to Ephesians 5:25. How could a man *leave* his wife and children and still be in God's will?

Some scholars believe that Jesus is talking about a man's response to God's initial "call" to salvation. Certainly, we must be willing to give up everything dear to us if it means our salvation. But regardless of how you interpret Jesus' reply to Peter, keep in mind that God never intended for a man to forsake his wife and children.

In the apostle Paul's first letter to Timothy, he said that a man who doesn't provide for his family has "denied the faith, and is worse than an infidel" (I Timothy 5:8). And God certainly never meant for a man to divorce his wife in order to follow God's calling. That kind of thinking belies everything Jesus ever said about marriage. (See Matthew 5:32; 19:6; Mark 10:11; Luke 16:18.)

My husband works with a gentleman whose wife was recently diagnosed with a rare condition that will ultimately render her unable to perform ordinary physical tasks. Because of his wife's condition, this man is taking early retirement, in order to give his wife the best life she can have for as long as possible. This kind of sacrificial love is what Paul is speaking of in his writings.

We've talked in general terms so far, but let's take a detailed look at the husband's role. Drawing from the "Building a Partnership" series and using Scripture as the authority, I've designed the following chart. It lists the husband's responsibilities, related scriptures, and the negative effects on a wife if a husband fails to fulfill his responsibility. Consider this *watering, feeding, weeding,* and *pruning* guidelines for marriage.

Husband's Responsibilities	Related Scriptures	Negative Effects on Wife if Husband Neglects This Responsibility
Take care of her. Make her needs a priority.	Ephesians 5:25: "Husbands, love your wives, even as Christ also loved the church, and gave himself for it."	Feels insecure, lonely, unloved, unimportant, unappreciated. As a result, wife may look elsewhere for needs to be met.
Respect your wife as an equal *partner* in Christ.	I Peter 3:7: "Husbands, . . . be considerate as you live with your wives, and treat them with respect . . . as heirs with you . . . so that nothing will hinder your prayers" (NIV).	Feels resentment, hurt, lack of confidence, inferior. As a result, wife may stop communicating, becoming withdrawn and depressed.
Value your wife's strengths, remembering God made her to be your *helper,* not your servant. Draw on her knowledge and insights, instead of discounting her ideas.	Genesis 2:18: "And the LORD God said, It is not good that the man should be alone; I will make him an help meet for him." Proverbs 18:22: "Whoso findeth a wife findeth a good thing, and obtaineth favor of the LORD."	Feels she's looked upon as little more than a housekeeper. As a result, wife may lose her self-respect, assume a "don't care" attitude, or erect walls around herself.
Compliment your wife for the unique person she is. *Appreciate* the talents and wisdom she possesses.	Proverbs 31:10: "Who can find a virtuous woman? for her price is far above rubies." Proverbs 19:14: "A prudent wife is from the LORD."	Feels she isn't valuable to you. Compares herself to other women. As a result, wife may try to gain attention of other men, due to her feelings of inadequacy.

Forgive your wife for her failures and offenses.	Mark 11:25: "And when ye stand praying, forgive, if ye have ought against any: that your Father also which is in heaven may forgive you your trespasses."	Questions husband's walk with God. Is unable to look at him as a spiritual leader. As a result, wife may become rebellious and defensive.
Admit wrongdoings and *accept* responsibility for your actions.	James 5:16: "Confess your faults one to another, and pray for one another, that ye may be healed."	Spirit becomes wounded, lacks humility toward, and submission to, husband. As a result, wife loses respect for husband and may develop a "coolness" toward him. What husband says goes in one ear and out the other.
Perform duties around the house and *assist* wife when needed.	Ephesians 5:25: "Husbands, love your wives, even as Christ also loved the church, and gave himself for it."	Feels husband doesn't appreciate family and home and doesn't value her work within the home. As a result, wife may let housework go.
Be *patient* and *understanding* when your wife doesn't please you.	I Corinthians 13:4: "Charity suffereth long, and is kind."	Is hesitant to share even small things with her husband, for fear of being misunderstood and condemned. Stops trying to please husband altogether.
Be *faithful*	Matthew 19:6: "What therefore God hath joined together, let not man put asunder."	Feels totally humiliated and debased. Unfaithfulness produces extreme anger and hurt that often causes the wife to leave her husband. Only the strongest of the strong can survive infidelity.

The Role and Obligations of Wives

It has long been my opinion that the majority of women have no trouble submitting themselves to their husbands, as long as their husbands are fulfilling their obligations to them, as outlined previously. In fact, most women I know would follow their husbands off a cliff, if he loved them unconditionally and treated them in the way God intended.

But let's face it. Even though a husband's duty is to love his wife unconditionally, his role is much easier if his wife is lovable.

Regrettably, not all women are lovable. They wake up complaining and go to bed complaining. They find fault with everything their husband does. They seldom have a kind word, and their idea of a compliment is saying, "Well, at least you didn't forget," when their husband gives them an anniversary present. They think their husband was put on the face of the earth to meet every need they ever have—and then some. And when he doesn't, they make sure they remind him of it as often as possible.

Dear friend, if you see a picture of yourself in the above paragraph, please don't get angry and slam this book shut. God wants to bring real change into your life and into your marriage. It is His desire that you have a harmonious relationship with your husband, but you can only do that if you are willing to accept your God-given responsibilities in marriage.

Maybe you're thinking that you'd be delighted to do your part if only that stubborn man of yours would do his. I hear you loud and clear, but God's instructions to wives aren't predicated on whether or not the husband is fulfilling his obligations. Even if your husband does not love you unconditionally, you have a duty to him. Ephesians 5:22-24 says, "Wives, submit yourselves unto your own husbands, as unto the Lord. For the husband is the head of the wife, even as Christ is the head of the church: and he is the saviour of the body. Therefore as the church is subject unto Christ, so let the wives be to their own husbands in every thing."

Drawing from the "Building a Partnership" series and using Scripture as the authority, I've designed the following chart. It lists the wife's responsibilities, related scriptures, and the negative effects on a husband if a wife fails to fulfill her responsibility. Consider this *watering, feeding, weeding,* and *pruning* guidelines for marriage.

Wife's Responsibilities	Related Scriptures	Negative Effects on Husband if Wife Neglects This Responsibility
Yield to his authority.	Ephesians 5:22: "Wives, submit yourselves unto your own husbands, as unto the Lord."	Feels like he has no control in the home. May become withdrawn or belligerent.
Regard him with great *honor.*	Ephesians 5:33: "Nevertheless let every one of you in particular so love his wife even as himself; and the wife see that she reverence her husband."	Feels belittled and unimportant. May seek female attention outside the marriage.

93

Be *agreeable*, easy to get along with, not demanding your own way.	Ephesians 5:22 (see previous page) Proverbs 21:19: "It is better to dwell in the wilderness, than with a contentious and an angry woman." See also Proverbs 21:9; 19:14	Begins to view wife in a negative way, even as a troublemaker. May start to point out her physical flaws as a counter to wife's tirades, which only makes things worse.
Be *diplomatic* and *tactful* in your communication.	Titus 2:5: "[Wives should] be discreet, chaste, keepers at home, good, obedient to their own husbands." Proverbs 31:26: "She openeth her mouth with wisdom; and in her tongue is the law of kindness."	Feels threatened and intimidated in conversations with wife. May stop talking altogether.
Be *faithful*.	Proverbs 31:11-12: "The heart of her husband doth safely trust in her . . . she will do him good and not evil." Titus 2:5 (see above)	Feels totally humiliated and debased. Unfaithfulness produces extreme anger and hurt that often causes the husband to leave his wife. Only the strongest of the strong can survive infidelity.
Maintain an orderly home.	Proverbs 31:27: "She looketh well to the ways of her household, and eateth not the bread of idleness."	A man's home is his castle. If it is a pigpen, he may become frustrated and irritable, or withdrawn and sulky. Or he may take on this responsibility, which only intensifies his bad feelings.
Be *patient* and *understanding* when your husband doesn't please you.	I Corinthians 13:4: "Charity suffereth long, and is kind."	Is hesitant to share his feelings with his wife for fear of being misunderstood and condemned. May stop trying to please wife altogether.

Forgive your husband for his failures and offenses.	Mark 11:25: "And when ye stand praying, forgive, if ye have ought against any: that your Father also which is in heaven may forgive you your trespasses."	Questions wife's walk with God. As a result, husband may continue his unseemly ways as revenge for his wife's unforgiving spirit.

Making a Marriage Last

Keeping a flower garden thriving, year after year, requires perpetual care and attention. It requires a keen eye, recognizing a problem early on, then seeking out and applying the necessary remedies.

Interestingly enough, each year generally produces a different set of problems in the world of gardening. One year may bring an invasion of slugs, while another year may be spent fighting white flies and aphids. There may be seasons of rain, or a season of drought. But regardless what malady the year brings, as long as you're committed to your garden and willing to do whatever is necessary to make it last, your garden will most likely survive.

Sometimes marriages need professional Christian counselors to help them survive. As I mentioned in an earlier chapter, when our cars break down, we take them to the auto shop. We should treasure our marriages much more, making sure we do all we can to make them whole whenever they are falling apart.

Ultimately, the same thing that keeps gardens alive will keep marriages alive, and that is one simple word: *commitment*. If you are *committed* to your spouse, nothing but death can tear you apart.

Summary

Some folks purchase healthy bedding plants, stick them in the ground, and pray for a miracle. It ain't gonna happen. Without constant TLC, the plants will die. And so it is with our marriages. If we want them to flourish, we must be willing to put in the necessary work. I'm convinced that God will honor our efforts to hold our marriages together.

step 7 | mend the fences—
keeping our boundaries intact

> *Remove not the ancient landmark,*
> *which thy fathers have set.*
> *— Proverbs 22:28*

One sunny Saturday, I was helping my neighbor prepare a plot of ground for a flower bed. In an attempt to separate the bed from the rest of the yard, we needed to define a border. We planned to dig up about four inches of the surface, then we'd build up the area with the needed topsoil and nutrients before planting.

As I stuck the shovel into the ground, it only went down about two inches before striking something hard. Kathy and I were amazed to discover a narrow row of old bricks buried there beneath the grass, some bearing twenty-year-old dates on them.

Probably, in years past, these bricks had served as a border for a thriving flower bed. But through years of disregard and inattention, what once had been visible had been trampled down until it had disappeared.

And therein lies the downfall of many would-be gardeners. You see, it's fairly simple to create a flower bed, but the tough part comes in maintaining the borders.

The same holds true for our spiritual borders. If we aren't diligent in preserving the borders that separate us from the world, before you know it, the distinction becomes less and less. We begin to look and behave just like everyone else.

Why We Need Fences

Fences serve two purposes: They keep things in, and they keep things out. By setting boundaries for ourselves and our families, we are attempting to keep the things we value safe. If we don't have fences, we give the enemy an open door to our homes, where he will steal the things that belong to us.

As we get closer to the second coming of Jesus Christ, the evil one has moved closer to our property, pressing hard upon the fences we have built for protection. Without question, only the strongest of fences will survive his onslaught. That's why we must quickly repair any cracks in our fences before the enemy discovers them and seizes the opportunity to rob us.

A Look Back

If you've studied history at all, you'll readily agree that the world we live in today is quite different from that of our parents' generation. This is a society of permissiveness. "If it feels good do it." "Let it all hang out." "Live and let live." "Life is short; party hard." The things we used to hold sacred and private are now on public display.

Walk into any junior department in any fashion store and much of the attire you will see on the racks looks as if it belongs on a prostitute. Skimpy and tight, with a suggestive slogan across the front, is what's selling as T-shirts these days. The more skin that shows, the better. It doesn't end there.

Ten to fifteen years ago, you would never walk into a fashion store and find women's lingerie lining the center aisle. Lingerie was considered a private matter, surrounded by an air of feminine mystique. Today, you can't go anywhere without it being displayed in an in-your-face style for every member of the family to behold. This is a sign that somewhere along the way, the fence between what is private and what is public has crumbled.

When the "I Love Lucy" show first aired in 1952, I am told that the producers would not allow any scene between Lucy and Desi Arnaz that showed them in the same bed. Although their characters were married to each other, they were always seen in twin beds, in modest pajamas.

Today, television is quite different. According to my research, not only are the characters in most of the shows not married to each other, they are often seen engaging in sexual activities, wearing little or no clothing.

This is yet another sign that a border has been trampled.

Why Fences Break

Have you ever driven by a cattle rancher's property and found a cow grazing along the highway? My guess is that somewhere there is a weakness in the fence. It may take a serious accident before the rancher even realizes there's a problem.

Breaks in our spiritual fences often happen subtly as well. We don't always notice it right away.

In 1993, while working for a large Houston corporation, a group of co-workers got together and formed a Christian network. Heading it up was Bill, an earnest young man who belonged to a large Baptist church. Each week, Bill sent an e-mail to the members of the network, encouraging us in our walk with God or sharing some insight from the Bible.

I still have in my filing cabinet the note Bill sent one Tuesday morning, and I will never forget how I wept when I read his stirring words.

"What are you saying when you say you believe in Jesus," he wrote, "yet you continue to watch the same garbage on TV as non-believers, continue to go to the same movies as non-believers, continue to dress immodestly like non-believers, continue to tell the same kinds of jokes and stories as non-believers, don't study the Bible, don't ever pray, don't ever want to talk about Jesus, don't care about all your friends who are going to hell because they don't believe in Jesus, turn a blind eye to the cries of the poor, the oppressed, the sick, and the prisoners, and continue to live a life that is totally indistinguishable from that of a non-believer?"

Here was a young man who clearly understood the need for separation from the world, and yet, sadly, many so-called Christians condone the very things Bill spoke out against.

Why?

Let's take a look at two of the reasons our fences get trampled down. Probably the number one reason—and this sounds a bit harsh—is pure laziness. It is just plain hard work to keep clear-cut boundaries in our lives and to be disciplined enough to enforce those boundaries. This is especially true if you have children.

When children are small, it's a piece of cake. You're in charge of every aspect of their lives. They go where you go. They do what you tell them to do. But as they grow up, becoming more and more independent, they want to do more things, be with more people, make new friends, and go more places. And it's not easy when you have to be the "hall monitor" day in and day out. There are times when you feel like all you say is no, no, no. Some days you just want to throw your hands up and surrender to whatever it is they are begging to do.

I remember reading a story several years ago about a mother who was having trouble with her teenage daughter wanting to wear a leather miniskirt. The daughter argued vehemently that everyone else was wearing them, so why couldn't she wear one?

With a voice as calm as a summer rain, the mother said, "I'm sorry, but the answer is no." On and on the argument went, and every time the mother repeated her mantra: "I'm sorry, but the answer is no."

Finally, in a fit of anger, the daughter stormed off to her room where she cried and screamed, all in an effort to break her mother down. Again, she came downstairs and inquired about the skirt, and, again, her mom said, "I'm sorry, but the answer is no."

Some time later, an odd thing happened. The girl broke down in tears and told her mother how glad she was that she remained firm in her resistance. She said, "I was so afraid that you were going to let me win."

If this diligent mother had been lazy, she would have given in to her daughter's demands, bringing another brick in the fence crashing down: "Wear whatever makes you feel good, honey. If the rest of the girls are doing it, I guess it must be OK." May God give us more parents with the tenacity of bulldogs.

Another reason fences crumble is because of peer pressure. Let's face it. Whether you're an adult or a child, it isn't easy being the only blackberry in a bowl of buttermilk.

In earlier times, you could tell just by observing whether or not people claimed to be Christians. They dressed differently. They talked differently. They didn't visit the places that non-Christians visited. They attended church often. They refrained from harmful habits and activities. In essence, they lived disciplined lives.

But as time went on, ministers began preaching a diluted message. What used to be black and white became gray. A straight line became zigzagged. What was once unacceptable became accepted. Voices of the world started calling to Christians. Don't be so stringent, they said. Lighten up. Some of those things you do aren't necessary in order to be a Christian. Surely God isn't concerned with such trivial things?

The Argument for Fences

One thing is sure: the Bible has not changed. We can try to justify ungodly living and ungodly apparel all we want, but God isn't moved. We can claim ignorance, but it doesn't change the Word of God. And just because every church in the city condones a worldly lifestyle is no sign that it's acceptable or OK.

Jesus said in Matthew 7:21-23: "Not every one that saith unto me, Lord, Lord, shall enter into the kingdom of heaven; but he that doeth the will of my Father which is in heaven. Many will say to me in that day, Lord, Lord, have we not prophesied in thy name? and in thy name have cast out devils? and in thy name done many wonderful works? And then will I profess unto them, I never knew you: depart from me, ye that work iniquity."

There are few subjects in the Bible emphasized as much as separation from the world. Take a look at just a few scriptures that clearly point this out:

I John 2:15: "Love not the world, neither the things that are in the world. If any man love the world, the love of the Father is not in him."

Romans 12:2: "And be not conformed to this world: but be ye transformed by the renewing of your mind, that ye may prove what is that good, and acceptable, and perfect, will of God."

II Corinthians 6:14-17: "Be ye not unequally yoked together with unbelievers: for what fellowship hath righteousness with unrighteousness? and what communion hath light with darkness? and what concord hath Christ with Belial? or what part hath he that believeth with an infidel? and what agreement hath the temple of God with idols? for ye are the temple of the living God; as God hath said, I will dwell in them, and walk in them; and I will be their God, and they shall be my people. Wherefore come out from among them, and be ye separate, saith the Lord, and touch not the unclean thing; and I will receive you."
I Thessalonians 5:22: "Abstain from all appearance of evil."

I Peter 2:9: "But ye are a chosen generation, a royal priesthood, an holy nation, a peculiar people; that ye should shew forth the praises of him who hath called you out of darkness into his marvellous light."

Romans 12:1: "I beseech you therefore, brethren, by the mercies of God, that ye present your bodies a living sacrifice, holy, acceptable unto God, which is your reasonable service."

Titus 2:12: "Teaching us that, denying ungodliness and worldly lusts, we should live soberly, righteously, and godly, in this present world."

Galatians 6:7-8: "Be not deceived; God is not mocked: for whatsoever a man soweth, that shall he also reap. For he that soweth to his flesh shall of the flesh reap corruption; but he that soweth to the Spirit shall of the Spirit reap life everlasting."

The Bible is chock-full of many more similar instructions. Do we think we can simply ignore these straightforward scriptures, choosing to go on and satisfy our carnal desires, living and looking like the sinners we seek to convert, instead of living the disciplined life that is spelled out in God's Word? If we can, then we may as well set the Bible out for the next trash pick-up day.

Without boundaries in our personal lives, we cannot please God. Nothing is clearer in Scripture than that simple fact.

Establishing Our Fences

That brings us to a question that sometimes produces a lot of confusion and argument: Where do we draw the line between right and wrong?

I'm no spiritual giant, by any stretch of the imagination. There have been times when I've failed miserably in living up to the standards outlined in Scripture. So I have no intention of trying to tell you how you must live your life, where you must draw the lines between right and wrong. We are given pastors for the "perfecting of the saints" (Ephesians 4:12).

In addition, there are some things that are clearly spelled out in God's Word (modesty and temperance comes to mind). Other things aren't quite so clear. Even so, there is something we can do to help us know if something is right or wrong.

I remember a day when a young woman came to me and asked if I thought it would be a sin if she did a certain thing. Mind you, what she inquired about seemed very insignificant, but I wasn't about to give her an answer to a question that to her was serious. So I said, "Let me ask you some questions. (1) Why do you want to do it? (2) Will it make you feel closer to God or farther away from God? (3) Will you be breaking any commandments outlined in the Word of God? (4) Will it make you look more like a woman of the world or more like a woman of God?"

By the time she finished answering those questions, she knew what to do.

And that's how it is so much of the time. If you will examine your motives—first and foremost—you will usually have no trouble distinguishing between right and wrong. And once you do, dig a hole in the ground and drive in a fence post.

God's greatest desire is for you to live a victorious life. It is illogical to believe that He would make it so complicated and so difficult that nobody could succeed. That is not to say that living a separated lifestyle requires no effort on our part, or that it is easy. But it becomes easier whenever we develop a close relationship with Christ. We *want* to please Him. We *want* to be like Him. We remember the great sacrifice that He made for our salvation, and that makes anything we sacrifice seem trivial in comparison to what He gave up for us.

The only true way of knowing what is right and what is wrong is by reading the Bible for ourselves, asking God to open our understanding. God's Word is forever settled in heaven. It is the one thing that will judge us all.

I've always found it fascinating—if not amusing— whenever I speak to people about God's Word and they say, "Well, I just don't believe thus and so about this or that."

The stark truth of the matter is it doesn't make an ounce of difference what I believe or what you believe. What matters is what does the Word of God have to say? If the Word of God negates my personal philosophy, then I'm just going to have to lay down my personal philosophy. The Word of God is the ultimate truth.

God has equipped all of us with a conscience—a sense of right and wrong. You know that little voice that talks to you whenever you've done something you know is wrong? That's your personal minister, sent by God to keep you on the straight and narrow path. Take heed that you don't ignore that little voice, for the more you ignore it, the softer the voice becomes.

If we are praying and studying the Word of God, if we are being discipled by a seasoned minister of God, and if we let our conscience guide us, I have no doubt that we will live in the way God wants us to. That doesn't mean it will always be easy. It hurts when we have to crucify our flesh, denying our worldly desires and lusts, forsaking the pleasures of sin. But it was the apostle Paul who said he died *daily* (I Corinthians 15:31). That says to me that Paul fought his flesh every day. He was no different than any of us. Every day he had to find an altar somewhere and surrender to God's will and to God's commandments.

The only way we will ever live a victorious life is one day at a time. By having a *daily* walk with God, a *daily* giving of ourselves, and *daily* dying out to our fleshly desires, we will become stronger Christians, and our fences of separation will be strong.

Summary

Whenever our boundaries are trampled, we lose our hedge of protection, becoming open targets for Satan's attacks. Too often we lose our most precious possessions. Mending fences and maintaining them require hard work, but in the end it saves an awful lot of grief. It is a task that we must not ignore.

step 8 | reach out and touch someone— fulfilling the second greatest commandment

For I was hungry and you gave me nothing to eat,
I was thirsty and you gave me nothing to drink,
I was a stranger and you did not invite me in,
I needed clothes and you did not clothe me,
I was sick and in prison and
you did not look after me.
— Matthew 25:42-43 (NIV)

I used to love hearing my grandfather tell of "the good old days" when neighbors were neighborly. If a storm blew your fence down, neighbors helped you mend it. If the baby got sick, a neighbor fetched the doctor for you. People often dropped in with a fresh pie or a mess of butter beans, just for the sake of helping out a neighbor.

In John 13:35, Jesus said: "By this shall all men know that ye are my disciples, if ye have love one to another." He did not say that all men would know we were His disciples because of the way we dress or the way we worship or the way we comb our hair, but by the *love we show* to each other.

Let me ask you a simple question: Are you helping those in need?

Perhaps your argument is that you would be glad to do so, if only there was an outreach program at your church, if only there was an outreach minister who was in touch with charity organizations and could direct you to needy people in the community. You don't know how to help or who to help.

I believe that every church, no matter how big or small, should have an active outreach department. But if you are in a church that does not, at the end of this chapter, I'm going to give you some ideas to get you started in your personal outreach ministry. First, let me try to persuade you that reaching out and touching someone is as much a ministry to *you* as it is to those in need. Helping others, while not always an easy or pleasant task, should be seen as a blessing, instead of a burden. And when you do it from your heart, that is exactly what it will be to you.

It is important that I emphasize that a man or woman's first obligation is to his or her family's needs. I am not in any way suggesting that someone neglect the needs of his or her family in order to serve other people. That is not God's will. However, by this chapter's end, I think you will see that reaching out to others can be done in a number of ways—both great and small.

Is it easy helping other people? Not always. Volunteering our time and services is not something that appeals to our human nature. It take us out of our familiar surroundings. It usually means we have to give up some of the things we do for ourselves. But I'm convinced that helping others, when done in the spirit of love and compassion, is the key to true inner happiness.

Habitat for Humanity just celebrated its twenty-fifth anniversary as a Christian charity organization. In its twenty-five-year history, 100,000 houses have been built for those who had no hope of ever owning a home. And the wonderful part is that all 100,000 homes were built by volunteers—ordinary people like you and me! Habitat's founder and president, Millard Fuller, says that building houses for others is a "tangible expression to the love of God."

Let me share with you part of Habitat for Humanity's mission statement, taken from their website at www.habitatforhumanity.com:

Habitat's ministry is based on the conviction that to follow the teachings of Jesus Christ we must reflect Christ's love in our own lives by loving and caring for one another. Our love must not be words only—it must be true love, which shows itself in action. Habitat provides an opportunity for people to put their faith and love into action.

True love *"shows itself in action."* That is a powerful statement, and I believe it is this—*action*—that is part of the "reasonable service" Paul spoke about in Romans 12:1.

In Mark 12:29-31, Jesus said: "The first of all the commandments is, Hear, O Israel; The Lord our God is one Lord: and thou shalt love the Lord thy God with all thy heart, and with all thy soul, and with all thy mind, and with all thy strength: this is the first commandment. And the second is like, namely this, Thou shalt love thy neighbour as thyself. There is none other commandment greater than these."

But just who is our neighbor?

When Jesus answered this question in Luke 10:30-37, He related the story of a man we've come to know as the Good Samaritan, a story containing all of the ingredients required when reaching out and touching someone. Let's examine what these things are.

- **Touching someone may mean getting your hands dirty.**

The Good Samaritan had compassion on the man who had been robbed and beaten and left for dead, and he went to him, bound up his wounds, then picked him up and set him on his own beast. I'm certain this was not a pleasant experience. The man was dirty. He probably smelled bad. That is all part of the cost of loving our neighbor as ourselves.

- **Touching someone may cost you financially.**

The Good Samaritan paid the suffering man's hotel bill and promised to pay whatever else was needed when he returned from his trip. He also promised to pay his medical bills, not even asking what the cost would be.

- **Touching someone may take you out of your comfort zone.**

The Good Samaritan was on a journey when he came upon the dying man by the side of the road. He had plans. He had a life. I dare say he had other things to worry about. It would have been easy just to keep going. But compassionate people *respond* to tragedies with *action*, instead of just sighing and shaking their heads in sympathy. You see, not only did the Samaritan bind up the man's wounds and take him to a hotel, he postponed his trip and spent the night taking care of him (Luke 10:34-35). He put his personal needs aside. Whoever was waiting on him at the end of his journey would just have to wait. He saw a need and went out of his way to fill it.

Jesus said, "Go, and do thou likewise." What sobering words.

One-on-one Ministry

Perhaps you have been looking at the big picture. So many people. So many needs. So little time. But ministering to the needy is seldom done among the masses. Instead, it is done one-on-one. Remember: you aren't trying to change the whole world; you're trying to change one person's world.

While volunteering at a crisis pregnancy center in 1991, I met Rebecca—a thirty-year-old single woman with one child and one on the way. Rebecca's problems were many; there was no way I could resolve all of the personal issues she had in her life. But what I could do was be a friend to her, offer godly counsel to her, baby-sit for her, clean and redecorate her apartment for her, make sure she had clothes that fit her, drive her to doctor appointments, take her to church with me. And when she was threatened by a former boyfriend, I paid for her and her child to stay at a hotel, and I spent the night with them.

Was it easy being Rebecca's friend? Honestly, at times, it was maddening. Our friendship often seemed like a one-way street, but I had to keep remembering that she had so little to give, while I had so much. In time, I saw Rebecca come to know the Lord. I saw her baptized. Witnessing these events made all of the time and effort I had contributed to Rebecca worthwhile.

In Luke 6:35, Jesus said, "Do good, and lend, hoping for nothing again; and your reward shall be great."

Sometimes our reward is slow in coming. Helping another person often seems pointless and without results, but be assured that our effort often means much more than we could ever imagine.

When my daughter entered high school, I wanted to find a way to get more involved as a parent. The school counselor introduced me to their mentoring program, a program that pairs responsible adults with students who are considered to be on the verge of dropping out of school. We would meet on campus, every other Friday, during the lunch period. She gave me an application and told me to think about it.

I really didn't need to think about it. I knew, right away, that I wanted to do this. Call me weird if you will, but I have a genuine fondness for teenagers—especially those who have seemingly slipped through the cracks of society and been forgotten.

That evening, as I filled out the application, I was drawn to one question in particular: "Why do you want to be a mentor?" There was only a small space in which to write my answer, so I gave the edited version. But let me share with you the unedited account of why I volunteer a few hours a month, mentoring an at-risk student.

In her poignant book *Voices*, Beatrice Sparks interviewed four teenagers who talked candidly about their lives. Although this book is now out of print, it had a lasting effect upon me and upon how I live my life. The story of "Mark" was especially compelling.

Mark said he never felt loved as a child. His parents constantly fought and seemed to have little time for anyone's needs—except their own.

When he was ten, his mother was admitted to the hospital for various recurring health problems. Mark was sent to stay with his grandparents in Dallas.

While there, he fondly recalled going to Sunday school. "It was like peace and love and security and all the things I'd ever needed and wanted," he remembered. "I didn't want the meetings to ever end, didn't want to leave that nice, safe, comfortable feeling. I wished Mom and Dad would take us every Sunday." But Mark's parents had never taken him to church; they didn't believe in God.

When Mark's mother was released from the hospital, she promptly filed for a divorce from her husband. Mark—against his will—was forced to move with his father to New York City.

Things did not go well for Mark in the big city. His dad spent most of his time away from home, leaving Mark to his own devices. By the time he was fourteen, Mark was using drugs. It was not long before he ran away from home.

At the age of fifteen, while hitchhiking through New Mexico, Mark was picked up by what he called a "long-haired sicko in a van." When Mark would not get in the back of the van for "fun and games," the man pushed him out onto the highway.

Mark recalled being crumpled up on the shoulder of the road "crying like a baby." He said he wanted to die and wondered if he would, right there in that desert place.

Several cars drove by, but none stopped. Soon, under a scorching sun, Mark began to feel faint. On the side of the highway, with a broken stick, he scratched these words: "I love you." He said he wanted to pass away loving somebody.

"Anybody, anywhere, I love you," he wrote. "Please,

love me. Please, somebody love me." He said he remembered thinking that surely at least one person in the world had to love him.

Eventually Mark was rescued by a sheriff. Shortly after, he moved back to Texas to live with his mom, who had since remarried.

Mark recalled being happy for a while, but it wasn't long before the emptiness returned. The longing for love overwhelmed him. His thoughts turned to death.

In the epilogue of *Voices*, Ms. Sparks reveals what became of each teenager two years after she had interviewed him or her. Sadly, she discovered that Mark had committed suicide.

His suicide note was heartbreaking: "Dear Anybody," he wrote. "If anybody cares, please stop me. Please, please stop me! Please Dad . . . please Mom . . . please relatives . . . please teachers . . . please religious people . . . please God. I've needed you all. I still need you. Anybody, please . . . please help me."

Perhaps the most heartbreaking thing about Mark's tragic life is that during his interview with Ms. Sparks, two years before his suicide, he said these words: "If someone just knew and cared enough to protect us from ourselves for a couple of hours, or a couple of weeks, or whatever, I think most kids would make it through the dark lonely valleys in their lives."

What a powerful plea for help from the mouth of a desperate young man. But nobody answered the call.

So as I considered the question on the mentor application: "Why do you want to be a mentor?" I remembered

Mark, and I wrote, "Because I believe one person can make a difference."

Whether you are a mother, a father, a teacher, a pastor, an aunt, an uncle, a grandparent, a Sunday school teacher, a classmate, or a neighbor, remember this: the world is awash with boys and girls just like Mark. And they are all hoping for someone to help them make it through the "dark, lonely valleys" of their life. Could you be that one? *Would* you be that one?

Answering the Call

How long has it been since you have looked outside of your own needs and tried to fill the needs of someone else? Do you sit in your air-conditioned home, day after day, night after night, with no thought of those who are waiting for someone to minister to them? Do you attend church two or three times a week, mingling with your own little circle of friends who all think, act, and look like you do?

If that describes your life, dear friend, you are not fulfilling the second greatest commandment. Let me encourage you to look around for an opportunity that God has placed in your world. What about that person at work who seems a bit strange, the one who seems like such a misfit in society, the one who is always alone? Why not go out of your way to be a friend? Reaching out to someone does not have to be some great task, but can be a simple act of kindness.

Jeanne Boucher was at M. D. Anderson Hospital in Houston undergoing treatment for breast cancer. This particular morning, she was being taken by wheelchair to yet another chemo treatment. Jeanne had lost all of her hair, she could not control her vomiting or other bodily functions. Her face was swollen. She remembers smelling "bad." She says she was ugly and physically and emotionally bankrupt.

But as Jeanne was being wheeled to treatment that morning, an elderly man was walking down the hall toward her. Even though she had never seen him before, she could tell he was a patient at M. D. Anderson fighting his own battle with cancer.

As this man approached Jeanne, he stopped the wheelchair, knelt down beside her, and put his arms around her. As he hugged her very gently, he said, "Darlin', I sure hope you're feeling better tomorrow."

Here was a man who was in a fight for his life, a man who probably needed a little encouragement himself. Yet he chose to look outside of himself, he looked past his own struggles and had compassion on this woman in need. He could have done like the priest and the Levite and walked on the other side of the corridor. He could have merely nodded in her direction and kept on going, but he went to where she was.

Jeanne says that this man's gift of compassion that day gave her the will to keep going, to get through not only that day, but to look to the future when she could pass that gift to another person.

Our act of kindness can be as simple as preparing a meal. How often I have failed to do as Jesus commanded in Luke 14:12-14: "When thou makest a dinner or a supper, call not thy friends, nor thy brethren, neither thy kinsmen, nor thy rich neighbours; lest they also bid thee again, and a recompence be made thee. But when thou makest a feast, call the poor, the maimed, the lame, the blind: and thou shalt be blessed; for they cannot recompense thee: for thou shalt be recompensed at the resurrection of the just."

Giving of yourself is meant to change another's life, but it will also change your own, in ways you never imagined.

Ideas to get you started:

- Instead of a garage sale, bundle up all those items and give them to charity.
- Invite a widow or widower to eat dinner with your family one Sunday each month.
- Offer to baby-sit for a single parent.
- Consider becoming a foster parent.
- Mentor an at-risk student.
- Gather blankets and non-perishable foods and take them to a homeless shelter.
- Become a volunteer for organizations like Meals on Wheels, Big Brother and Big Sister, or Birthright.
- There are dozens of organizations that need people to help out just two or three hours a week. Check the Yellow Pages under "volunteer programs," or call a local radio or TV station to find out about charitable organizations in your area.

Summary

Something mysterious occurs when you reach out and touch another person. Instead of thinking about your expanding girth, the shape of your nose, or the fact that you inherited your mother's hips, you feel at peace. The great humanitarian Albert Schweitzer said, "I do not know what your destiny will be, but one thing I know: The only ones among you who will be really happy are those who will have sought and found how to serve." Perhaps Mr. Schweitzer is right: Serving others may be the only way to uncover the excellence within ourselves.

step 9 | relax in your favorite chair—
understanding the benefits of resting

And he rested on the seventh day from all
his work which he had made.
— Genesis 2:2

Are you getting enough rest? I don't mean the kind where you rest your head against the back of the car seat at red lights. I'm talking about an extended rest, when you don't answer the phone, you don't turn on the computer, you don't do laundry, you don't go shopping. All you do is rest.

Resting is not a priority for many people. They claim they don't have time to rest. They are caught up in the mind-set that we need to fit as many activities into our daily lives as there are waking hours. We sign our children up to play a myriad of sports, then spend hours on the roads, shuttling them back and forth. We agree to make homemade brownies for the fourth-grade Christmas party, when the boxed kind would have worked just as well. We volunteer to make a dozen craft projects for the fall bazaar, when we know Aunt Ida and Uncle Bill are coming for their yearly visit. In short, we run ourselves ragged trying to accomplish the impossible.

How is it that fifty years ago, we had the same twenty-four hours in a day, there were no dishwashers, no microwaves, no computers, no fax machines, no cellular telephones, no pagers, no disposable diapers, and yet people drove slower and found time to sit on the front porch after a long day's work?

All of our modern devices are meant to save us time. But instead of using this extra time to relax and enjoy loved ones, we often take on more and more responsibilities, producing more stress in our lives, giving us less time to rest.

According to the National Sleep Foundation, a lack of adequate rest can create all sorts of problems. Here are just a few:

- Difficulty concentrating
- Increased feelings of stress
- Inability to handle minor irritations
- Inability to perform tasks involving memory or logical reasoning
- Increased absence from work
- Psychiatric problems
- Increased risk of accidents—at home, on the job, and on the road

Too much stress and not enough rest can also create serious health problems. Doctor Redford Williams, a behavioral medicine expert at Duke University Medical Center, says there is a strong connection between stress and poor health. "What stress does, in all different forms, is lower resistance to all pathogens," he says. "This leaves people more susceptible to infections and even some cancers."

Our example for living is Jesus Christ. If you study the life of Christ, you will discover that He was never in a hurry. He took time to rest, to talk to children, to get away from the crowds, to be alone with His Father. And God understands our need for rest.

In one of her many devotional books, Mrs. Charles E.

Cowman relates the story of Elijah. If you recall, this prophet spent an exhausting day upon the mountain, all in an effort to prove to Ahab and to all the people that Baal was a false god and that Yahweh was the only one true God. He was doing the Lord's work, as we say. (See I Kings 18.)

But that wasn't all Elijah did that day. After fire fell from heaven, proving that Baal was a false god and that Yahweh was the only one true God, the Bible says that Elijah climbed to the top of Mount Carmel and prayed for rain. Not once. Not twice. But seven times he prayed for rain. And when the Lord answered by sending a small cloud, Elijah was so convinced that rain was coming that he told his servant to tell Ahab that he'd better hitch up the chariot and get down the mountain before the rains stopped him.

The Bible then says that the power of the Lord came upon Elijah and he outran Ahab's chariot.

What an exhilarating and victorious day! Many folks might read that account and think that Elijah should be on top of the world after that. But if you read the next chapter, you will find that Elijah is exhausted, afraid, depressed, and hiding. Well, well. He was human, after all. And the beautiful thing about this whole story is that God not only understood, but sent angels to minister to Elijah and to feed him because "the journey is too great for thee" (I Kings 19:7).

If you are weary and depressed, don't think of it as a sign of spiritual weakness. It is a sign of your humanity, and your Creator understands you need consistent rest and refreshing.

One of my favorite poems was written by Ella Conrad

Cowherd and appears in *Streams in the Desert* by Mrs. Charles E. Cowman:

> I'm too tired to trust and too tired to pray,
> Said one, as the over-taxed strength gave way.
> The one conscious thought by my mind possessed,
> Is, oh, could I just drop it all and rest.
>
> Will God forgive me, do you suppose,
> If I go right to sleep as a baby goes,
> Without an asking if I may,
> Without ever trying to trust and pray?
>
> Will God forgive you? why think, dear heart,
> When language to you was an unknown art,
> Did a mother deny you needed rest,
> Or refuse to pillow your head on her breast?
>
> Did she let you want when you could not ask?
> Did she set her child an unequal task?
> Or did she cradle you in her arms,
> And then guard your slumber against alarms?
>
> Ah, how quick was her mother love to see,
> The unconscious yearnings of infancy.
> When you've grown too tired to trust and pray,
> When over-wrought nature has quite given way:
>
> Then just drop it all, and give up to rest,
> As you used to do on a mother's breast,

He knows all about it—the dear Lord knows,
So just go to sleep as a baby goes;

Without even asking if you may,
God knows when His child is too tired to pray.
He judges not solely by uttered prayer,
He knows when the yearnings of love are there.

He knows you do pray, He knows you do trust,
And He knows, too, the limits of poor weak dust.
Oh, the wonderful sympathy of Christ,
For His chosen ones in that midnight tryst,

When He bade them sleep and take their rest,
While on Him the guilt of the whole world pressed—
You've given your life up to Him to keep,
Then don't be afraid to go right to sleep.

Sometimes it takes us awhile to learn how to slow down when we're accustomed to constant activity. The following ideas are intended to inspire you to do just that, making time for genuine relaxation in your busy lives. Some of these suggestions may appeal to you, while others may not. The most important thing to remember is that if you're doing the same old things and seeing the same old results, it's time to try something different.

Create a Reasonable Schedule

When I was working forty hours a week, it didn't take me long to realize that the old cliché "A woman's work is never done" is true. After eight hours on the job, not counting the commute, I came home to another job: a household that needed constant care.

Luckily, I have a terrific husband who has always helped out around the house, but—with all due respect—there are some things women do better than men. And there are some things women believe they must do in order to live with themselves. However, when I came home from work, I was generally too tired to want to do more than was absolutely necessary. All household tasks—including laundry—tended to be pushed to the weekend, which meant that my weekends were spent huffing and puffing, trying to get it all done before Monday morning. There had to be a better way.

When I complained to a co-worker one Monday about my state of exhaustion, she suggested I put myself on a work schedule at home, then post the schedule on the refrigerator where I wouldn't forget. I couldn't believe how this one simple act changed my life and left my weekends totally free of must-do chores.

Below is an example of what my schedule looked like. It does not include less-frequent jobs, like washing windows, taking drapery down and cleaning it, or wiping down baseboards and walls. It also does not include tasks like preparing dinner or running errands, which can often be done as a "team" effort with other family members.

Starting the evening's chores as soon as I arrived home worked best for me. Laundry could wash while I prepared dinner. If I waited too long, I was tempted to put it off until the next day.

Set up your schedule to suit your activities and needs. Tip: If you have children, assign them at least one chore per day.

Monday – dust and vacuum entire house, do one load of laundry, water indoor plants as needed, pick up rooms (meaning anything that doesn't belong in the room is returned to its place).

Tuesday – clean bathrooms (mop floors, clean toilets, tubs, and mirrors), do two loads of laundry, pick up rooms.

Wednesday – do "easy" load of laundry. (I usually wash towels and washcloths on Wednesday nights, as they can stay in the dryer without wrinkling. I could fold them after church, if necessary.)

Thursday – clean out refrigerator, clean kitchen appliances, mop kitchen and laundry room floors, do two loads of laundry, pick up rooms.

Friday – dust and vacuum entire house, do laundry as needed, pick up rooms.

Saturday – Rest from all labor!

Sunday – Attend church.

Even though I no longer work forty-hour weeks, I find that keeping myself on a schedule is still beneficial, and I think you will, too.

Limit Obligations

Another way we can find more time for relaxation is by limiting our obligations. Learning to say no is difficult for many people. They fear they will be ridiculed or that somebody will stop liking them. They want to please everyone at all times. They believe they are disappointing God whenever they say no to helping out in every church and school function that comes along.

I'm all for getting involved in church activities and community projects. The previous chapter in this book is about giving of ourselves to others. The secret lies in knowing how to prioritize and limit your commitments so you are effective.

For example, if you teach Sunday school, organize fellowships, work in the nursery, serve on the youth committee, sing in the choir, direct school plays, volunteer at a crisis pregnancy clinic, deliver meals to senior citizens, teach a weekly Bible study, and head up the ladies' auxiliary, you're stretching yourself dangerously thin.

There is no way you can be successful at anything when you try to do it all. There's nothing wrong with not being able to do it all. You are, after all, one person. You have limitations. How much better it is when you focus on a specific area. Not only will you be more successful, you will be able to schedule time for rest and relaxation without feeling guilty.

Stop Trying to be Perfect

No doubt you've heard the saying, "Nobody's perfect." Still, it doesn't keep some of us from trying. I know one woman who vacuums her entire 3,500-square-foot house daily, including pulling the sofas away from the walls. She obsesses about every speck of dust and every smudged windowpane. And she works a full-time job to boot. I often feel sorry for her. Even she has admitted that she has lost the joy of living.

Trying to be perfect can drive you and your family bonkers. It also leaves little room for anything else in your life—including a relationship with God. If we were perfect, we would have no use for God's mercy, grace, forgiveness, or help.

One of my favorite verses of Scripture comes from Psalm 6:2, where David says, "Have mercy upon me, O LORD; for I am weak." I have often quoted this verse during the course of my day. I am *weak*. I am *not perfect*. I *can't* be perfect. I am *human*. I *can't* do it all. *Lord, I need your help.*

All of our strength comes from God, and it's OK to acknowledge our weakness. It is when we are at our weakest that God will be His strongest.

If you struggle with perfectionism, I encourage you to ask God to help you learn a better way. It is not His will that you go through life worrying and stressed out. The Bible is filled with scriptures that admonish us to "wait patiently," to "rest in the Lord," to "be still."

There are a number of ways you can better your life and get the victory over a perfectionist attitude. Begin by asking for help from family members. Children can fold towels or set a table. The job may not be done to perfection, but resist the urge to correct their mistakes. Resist the urge to criticize their efforts.

I remember the first time I asked my daughter to fold a load of towels for me. She was about six at the time and the results were lopsided and uneven—a perfectionist's nightmare. But just as I was about to offer assistance, the thought hit me right between the eyes: It's just a towel, for crying out loud! What difference does it really make how it's folded under the counter? Who will see it?

I was pleasantly surprised at the relief that came when I forced myself to accept her less-than-perfect attempt. It was OK. It was *really* OK. And I am happy to report that I no longer worry about how the towels are folded.

When you learn to let others do things around the house, you may not get perfection, but it's one less thing you'll have on your to-do list, and it takes you one step closer to that comfy recliner where you can put your feet up for a time of pure rest.

Rethink Vacation Habits

When we're convinced we cannot go another mile on our runaway treadmill, we often decide a vacation is exactly what the doctor ordered. So we eagerly plan a little time of R&R. You know what that stands for, don't you? Rest and Relaxation.

But seldom does it work that way. What usually happens is our vacation mirrors our daily lives—packed to capacity with activities. We come home more tired than when we left. It takes us a week to unwind from the vacation that was supposed to unwind us.

If I've just rung your bell, maybe you need to rethink your vacation habits. Maybe you should even consider a *radical* change.

Before I married, if you had asked me if I wanted to

go camping, I would have said you were nuts. Only weird people went camping. But two years after our marriage, we borrowed a truck from my husband's father, borrowed a travel trailer from a trusty friend, and drove to the breathtaking beaches of Destin, Florida, where we camped for a week. The following year, we drove there again, only this time we pitched a tent next to my sister and brother-in-law's little pop-up camper. A few years later, we went back and stayed in a rustic beachside cabin. Today, we own a thirty-foot travel trailer and, if we're lucky, we enjoy camping-out several times a year.

Camping is something I never thought I would enjoy, and if my husband had not insisted I try it, I never would have known the pleasure that it can bring. The rewards of being in the outdoors surprised me. There was an amazing calm that took place in my spirit—both night and day.

Instead of rushing to get into a hotel elevator to go to breakfast every morning, I stepped out into the morning air, plugged in a pot of coffee and pulled out a skillet. In the evenings, instead of being squashed in a tiny hotel room, there was an entire world, just waiting to be enjoyed. And nothing is quite so peaceful as sitting on a little porch or gathering around a campfire while counting the stars in a velvet night sky.

Not only is camping-out a wonderful time for relaxing in an unhurried environment, it is also a great time for family bonding.

Gary Smalley, founder and president of Today's

Family, an organization which sponsors family enrichment seminars nationwide, and author of *The Key to Your Child's Heart*, talked with numerous "unusually happy" families across the country. Interviewing each family member alone, Smalley discovered one activity in common: camping.

There does seem to be something magical about the great outdoors. I recall our trip to the Great Smoky Mountains in 1994. One night, as we sat around the campfire, talking and studying the heavens, my little daughter—then eight—said, "Mama, I'm having the funnest time I've ever had." The sincerity in her voice has stayed with me all these years.

You don't have to travel to the Great Smoky Mountains in order to enjoy a "vacation" outdoors. Consider a weekly nature hike. Let the children take along a plastic bag or a bucket and collect interesting objects from their excursions. I have a lovely assortment of rocks, peach seeds, acorns, seashells—all from walks with my daughter.

Another idea is to pack a picnic lunch on Saturday and head to a local park. Take along books, sporting equipment, blankets, and a radio. Such brief outings often bring long-term rewards. You'll discover the unmatched feeling of lying flat on your back on an old quilt, staring into the vast heavens, and your children will make memories to treasure for years to come.

Find Small Ways to Rest

If you don't have large slices of time in which to rest,

don't fret. There are countless small ways to grab a few minutes for regrouping and refueling your energies. Here are a few:

- Soak your worries away in an extended candle-lit bath.
- Spend an hour at a local library, thumbing through old magazines.
- Create a special "corner" in your home for quiet times. A comfortable chair, a small table for holding books or beverages, a reading lamp, a scented candle, combined with an attractive throw for snuggling work just fine.
- Unplug the phone, turn on some soothing music, and recline on the sofa for at least thirty minutes.
- Sit outside and watch a sunrise or sunset.
- Lie flat on your back in the grass and gaze at the heavens for a solid fifteen minutes or until your eyes close.
- Get alone and count your blessings.
- Take an interesting book or magazine to a quiet coffee shop or diner. Request a back booth, order a favorite drink, and indulge to your heart's content.
- Talk your spouse into putting you up at a nearby hotel for a weekend stay. If spouse wants to come along, that's OK, too. Uninterrupted time together can be beneficial to both of you.

I've discovered that taking time to rest is not only advantageous for me, but for my family as well. I have more patience. I am more at peace. It feels as if all of the turmoil and pressures have been washed out of my soul. I feel cleansed somehow. Even when we go on vacations, I make sure I spend some time alone.

It was Anne Morrow Lindbergh who wrote, "Every person, especially every woman, should be alone sometime during the year, some part of each week, and each day. I find there is a quality to being alone that is incredibly precious. Life rushes back into the void, richer, more vivid, fuller than before."

Summary

It is easy to get so busy and so tangled up in the trappings of this present world that we lose sight of the daily miracles of life itself. We say we don't have time to rest, but even God rested. Making time for quiet and rest is essential in order to reap the joyful life God wants us to have.

recommended reading

At Home in My Heart, by Rebecca Barlow Jordan, (ISBN 1-58660-147-4)

Dare to Trust, Dare to Hope Again, by Kari West (ISBN: 0-7814-3587-0)

Deceived by Shame, Desired by God, by Cynthia Spell Humbert (ISBN: 1-57683-219-8)

How to Handle Adversity, by Charles Stanley (ISBN: 0-8407-9094-5)

Love Extravagantly, by Marita Littauer (ISBN: 0-7642-2276-7)

Prayerwalk: Becoming a Woman of Prayer, Strength, and Discipline, by Janet Holm McHenry (ISBN: 1-57856-376-3)

Seven Life Principles for Every Woman, by Sharon Jaynes & Lysa Terkeurst (ISBN: 0-8024-3398-7)